2nd Edition

15 Minutes to a Great Dog

Kevin Michalowski

©2006 Kevin Michalowski

Published by

kp books
An Imprint of F+W Publications

700 East State Street • Iola, WI 54990-0001
715-445-2214 • 888-457-2873

Our toll-free number to place an order or obtain
a free catalog is (800) 258-0929.

Library of Congress Catalog Number: 2005901826

ISBN: 0-89689-271-9

Designed by Kara Grundman

Printed in the United States of America

Dedication

To my boys, Adam and Ethan, who would have me buy every dog in the world and gladly help me care for them all.

Acknowledgments

This book wouldn't have gotten done without the prodding and sacrifices of my wife, Jackie. Thank you, my dear. Now you should have time to go riding.

Thanks also to Steve, Dan, Tracy, Sandi, Dean, M.D. and Julie, and everyone who put up with me as I used their dogs for photos.

Special thanks to Kellie at Cabela's and everyone at Doskocil for providing good, clean products to be photographed. Dog owners everywhere know that nothing stays clean for long, and the good-looking photos were really not my doing.

Kevin Howard, PR man extraordinaire, has helped me every step of the way, getting me in touch with Bob West and Dr. Arliegh Reynolds from Purina, whose knowledge of canine nutrition is second to none.

And let us not forget Echo, Oscar and Lucky, my wonderfully willing yellow Labradors, who put up with all sorts of indignity to show that they really did respond well to 15 minutes of training every day.

Him and Her

No, I'm not referring to the beagles owned by former U.S. President Lyndon Johnson; I'm talking about the masculine and feminine pronouns used throughout this book. I believe dog ownership is a very personal thing and really didn't want to go "gender-neutral" through the entire book. So, bear with me as you see pretty much random changes between him and her as I make reference to dogs in training.

I have no personal preference between male or female dogs. I like them all. I also know that you readers will be training dogs of both sexes, so I tried to alternate, just to keep everyone happy. You'll get the idea.

"I'm ready. Give me a command."

The Order of Things

Introduction

What does it take to get a great dog? Not as much as you'd think.

Have you ever seen a dog tugging at a leash, seeming to drag his owner around the block on the evening walk? Have you watched someone's playful pet jumping around, knocking over children as it completely ignores all who try to calm the animal? Or have you ever called a dog until you are red in the face and so completely frustrated that you wondered why you ever even thought to give food and shelter to such an ignorant beast? Most of these cases end with someone finally getting hold of the dog and sheepishly saying, "He just needs some training. I wish I had more time."

But how much time can you afford to devote? After all, you're busy. With jobs, kids, car repairs and home maintenance, and the never-ending, ever-growing list of things that make demands on your time, do you really have time to train a dog?

Yes, you do! And you can do it in just about 15 minutes a day.

It's true, 15 minutes a day is all it takes to train your dog. And you will be amazed at the results. That's because all dogs, young or old, registered show champion or refugee from the pound, have the capacity to learn. What makes it even easier is that most dogs want nothing more than to please their masters. So, if you want a great dog, read the first few pages of this book, gather up the few things you'll need and go get your dog. Before long, those days of yelling, hollering and questioning the dog's lineage and your good judgment will be gone forever. In just a short time people will begin to say, "What a great dog. Where did you find the time?"

Who knew that you had it all along? You just needed to know how to use it.

Kevin Michalowski
August 2005

A Word About Commands — Once

To train any dog, you will use commands. Put simply, commands are how we humans communicate with our dogs. Throughout this book I'll make reference to you issuing commands. Just about every chapter includes some sort of command. You need to think in the terms of giving orders. We should not be asking, begging or pleading with a dog. We should be telling the dog what to do and the dog should obey.

Yet everybody knows communication is never really that simple. Non-verbal clues, body language and voice inflection all play a huge part in how we communicate with other people, and especially with our dogs. Most communication between canines is silent. When the dominant dog of a pack wants to be the first to eat, the point is made without much noise. If the subordinate dog feels defiant, an escalation occurs until one animal backs down. If that doesn't happen, some fur could fly. But actual fights are rare. There's usually more posturing than there is real combat. When dealing with our canine friends, our commands should be direct, consistent and given clearly either by voice or by whistle. They should also be given once and only once, and they should be obeyed. After all, they are commands, not requests.

But how do we get to that point; that wonderful place where we give a command once, and that's all that we need to say? Well, you don't get there. You start there. From your earliest training sessions, you should give your command once, then make sure the dog complies. This, of course, is easier said than done. That's because it's human nature to want to repeat ourselves if we feel we are not heard. It's also true that when we start repeating ourselves, we also tend to increase the volume, hoping that what we have to say will eventually inspire the correct actions. If you have kids, you understand Bill Cosby's wonderful line, "Kids don't listen. So you repeat yourself until you end up sounding like a tobacco auctioneer, 'Sit down. Sit down. Sit. Sit! Sit! Sit… sit, down!'"

If you do something similar with your dog, all you are teaching that animal is that it doesn't have to respond on the first command. If the dog has even the slightest bit of a defiant streak in his personality, you can bet it will appear if you start to repeat your commands. Repeated commands teach a dog that it has only to respond on the fourth or fifth command, if it wants to respond at all. By repeating your commands, you are not advancing to the next level of dominance the way an alpha dog would in a wild pack. You need to up the stakes and do it right away. The two keys to nipping this situation in the bud are control and consistency.

Start with control. All early training, and any remedial training, must be done on the lead or a long check cord. This gives you total control and the ability to provide instant corrective action if your first command is greeted with a less than enthusiastic response. For instance, if the command "sit" is given and the dog does not immediately respond, you can pull up on the short lead, push down on the animal's butt and force compliance. This makes you the dominant one. Without the lead, you are just hoping the dog will

Don't repeat your commands; enforce them. When commanded to come, this dog has no choice but to comply.

respond. As a rule, use the lead until your dog complies perfectly every time you issue the command, then use it for another three weeks to a month.

Consistency is also important. If you demand "first-time, every-time" compliance in the yard during training, but resort to giving multiple commands elsewhere, your dog will quickly know what's happening and take advantage of the newfound freedom in precisely the place you want total control. If your dog happens to slip and fails to respond to a command, remember that the training is more important than the current activity. Stop what you are doing and force the issue. Be dominant. Call the dog to heel, snap on the lead and make the animal comply.

Dog training isn't difficult, but it does take some thought. If we slow down and think about what we are really doing and saying, we can create dogs that respond the first time, every time. This is done by quickly and clearly establishing your dominance.

And remember, we're not getting to that point in our training; we are requiring it right from the start.

Chapter 1

Getting Started

A Few Miscellaneous Things to Think About

Training a dog does not require a truckload of complicated gadgets. Truth be told, you could very likely get by with nothing more than a leash and lots of patience. But there are a few things you'll want to have to make your job easier. Before we get going on the lists of things you need and don't need, it's important to think about the kinds of things you'll be buying, and how they relate to your dog. Think of your dog-training gear like you'd think of clothes — these items need to fit your dog, not only the size of the animal, but the intended use as well. Your personal training style will dictate what type of items you buy, so think ahead. For example, do you really need the 40-foot retractable leash, or will the 6-foot nylon strap serve you well?

With that in mind, here's a list of basic equipment you'll want to consider purchasing when you start to train your dog.

These are the basics. You can train and care for a dog with surprisingly few items.

A good collar will be stout and fit well. This one also has a reflector for added safety after dark.

Collars

Measure the dog's neck and get a collar that fits. Collars are inexpensive, so buy the right size and replace worn collars right away.

Choke Collar

It's sometimes important for larger dogs, especially adult dogs that are going through remedial lessons, to be trained with the help of the choke collar. This chain loop is really just an attention-getter; you won't actually be choking the dog with it. Again, choose one that fits. They rarely wear out, so the only time you'll need to get a new one is if the dog grows out of it.

Check Cord

This is the long line used for controlling your dog from a distance. You can make one or buy one. Just remember, if you make one, don't buy really heavy rope. It can be too much for smaller dogs to pull around. Also, don't buy really light rope; you'll hate the effect it has on your hands if the dog decides to pull really hard.

Good whistles are inexpensive, and they really help with training. Get a couple of them.

When teaching your dog to fetch, use a tennis ball or dummies made for the activity. Throwing sticks for a dog is just not safe.

Whistles

There are several good brands of dog whistles out there. Choose one you like and buy a couple of them because they will get lost. Get a couple good whistle lanyards and keep the whistle around your neck so it's always handy during training. A whistle also makes a great conversation piece. When someone asks, "What's with the whistle?" you have the option of telling them if you're a dog trainer.

Dog Box

Often called a portable kennel, this serves as a training device, a dog bed and a safe means to transport the dog in a vehicle. Again, get the right size. If you have a puppy, get a small box and move up to a bigger box as the dog grows.

Chew Toys

Go with rawhide bones, that way you always have **the** right thing to offer the dog. The rawhide is good for **the dog's** teeth, is inexpensive and is fairly durable.

Fetch Toys

Buy tennis balls or dog-training dummies. Never throw a stick for your dog. A dog running with a stick is an accident looking for a place to happen. Cuts to the mouth and potential injuries to the throat may be severe and often require the attention of a veterinarian. Such an accident could cause the dog to avoid the game of fetch altogether. What fun would that be?

Bedding

Get the high-end doggie pillows from one of the big catalog retailers listed in the back of the book. Better quality will last longer, put up with more washings and be more comfortable.

A good dog bed needs to be tough and easy to clean. Cheaper beds that don't hold up will cost you more in the long run.

Food and water are the keys to your dog's health. Don't skimp. Buy the good stuff and keep the bowls clean.

Training Treats

I personally buy my training treats in bulk at the local wholesale club. There are all kinds of treats on the market today. You can find anything from high-energy, all-meat snacks to meat-free, all-veggie snacks in case you and your companion have recently turned vegetarian. Buy the kind your dog likes and argue the merits of their nutrition later. But, no matter what kind you buy, use them wisely.

Dog Food

Get the good stuff. While you can get away with bargain-basement food, your dog's health depends on the nutrition you provide. This is outlined nicely in Chapter 13. While it would be easy to recommend one brand and finish this paragraph, food selection is more complicated. Ask your veterinarian about the type of food your dog needs. Many vets will recommend the stuff they sell, but you can dig deeper. A great question is, "What type of food should my dog have?" Ask your vet to recommend the amount of protein your dog needs, how much fat is the right amount and what, if any, supplements you should provide.

Cleaning Gear

There is no hiding the fact that dogs do what dogs do. It's your unsavory responsibility to clean up afterwards. Whether you choose a shovel, the ever-popular Pooper Scooper or the ubiquitous plastic bag, get used to the fact that, to amend the street slang to a gentler term, feces occurs.

There are a whole host of other things that crafty marketers will convince you to buy. Before long, you'll end up with everything from dog brushes to flea powder to doggie toothpaste. Some of these items will turn out to be indispensable assets. Others will gather dust on your shelves. Sometimes it's difficult to keep from plunking down your hard-earned cash on something you're certain your dog "needs." On the other hand, unless you like buying stuff just because your canine companion needs a gift every now and then, ask your veterinarian. Chances are, your dog will do fine with reliable basic care, good quality food, fresh water and the kind of companionship and training only you can provide.

The question then becomes, "Are you ready to provide it?" I'll try my best to keep this from sounding like that lecture your parents gave you when you were 9 and "really, really, really, really" wanted that puppy. You promised to take care of him every day, clean up after him and walk him, "… and everything!"

Then your dad looked down at you and said, "Owning a dog is a big responsibility. It's a lot of work."

Bah! The dads who said that were the ones who didn't really want a dog in the first place. Owning a dog doesn't have to be and, indeed, shouldn't be a chore. It should be fun. The work you have to do should be completely overshadowed by the companionship the dog provides. If you follow the steps in this book and keep a positive attitude, the training will be fun. It won't even feel like work. You'll simply feel like you're playing with the dog. Then, before too long, the responses to your commands will be crisp and quick. You'll start to worry less and less about what your dog will do and think more and more about what you and your dog can do together.

If you own this book, chances are you probably already own a dog. That means you've made the commitment to care for and train the animal. My guess is you made that commitment thinking dog ownership would be a lot of work. Now that you're finding out it's really not all that much work, things will be easier than you ever imagined. So, let the fun begin.

Chapter 2

Training the Trainer

You don't have to shake your head and say, "I just don't have the time to work with that dog." That's because the first thing you need to know about dog training is that it doesn't take a lot of time. In fact, your dog will get more out of your training sessions if you keep them short.

If you're one of those people who think having a well-trained dog means hour upon hour of diligent training, think again. You can train your dog in 15 minutes a day. You just need to know how. There's no mystery involved. There's nothing truly amazing about the techniques of professional dog trainers. They issue simple commands, and they repeat the sequence until the dog's reaction to the command becomes second nature.

A few minutes of good basic training every day will give you a great dog.

To train your dog in basic obedience, all you really need to do is focus on the training for a few minutes each day. During that time you'll teach some basic commands and repeat them until the dog understands how you want things done. It's like building with blocks. Each block is the foundation for the next step. Follow the simple training tips presented in this book, and you will build a foundation of basic skills that will make your pet a joy to be around.

There's nothing difficult about training a dog. What can be difficult is **learning** to train a dog. It's not that the techniques are so tough or the commands so difficult to master; it's just that while you are training your dog, you've got to stop thinking in human terms. Dogs don't use logic or reason; they just respond. It's a simple case of action and reaction, and the dog learns through repetition.

It would be easy to say, "You've got to think like a dog." But we humans don't really know how dogs think. We do know how dogs react to what we do. They are pack animals and respond instinctively to every situation. We can observe changes in their posture and demeanor as we change the tone of voice we use, our own posture, our actions or even sometimes the looks on our faces. This is where

It's never too early to instill the concept of patient training. Even young dog trainers will get the idea if you demonstrate.

Whistle commands are clear and precise. The best part is you can be sure they are heard.

dog training really starts. It is about paying attention to how the dog reacts to what you do and say. Once you start to notice these things, then you can begin to modify a dog's behavior by showing the animal what you expect, giving a simple command, forcing the dog to comply and repeating the sequence (Notice I said repeating the sequence, not the command. More on that later.) until the action — actually the reaction to the command — becomes automatic.

Therefore, the first step in training a dog is to train the trainer. This begins and ends with patience. Patience will be your master while you are trying to teach your dog. Lose your patience and your training session will end. That is to say, if you are impatient or irritable, the training you hope to provide will stop, even if you double the amount of time you spend with your dog. On top of that, if you become impatient, your dog may be learning things you don't want her to learn. Then you will have to backtrack and remedy those "bad habits" before you move ahead, teaching the things that are really important.

Lost patience typically shows up as some sort of aggressive frustration on the part of the dog trainer. There are as many different manifestations of lost patience as there are dog owners in the world. The worst of these include shouting at, hitting, kicking or using the leash to beat your dog. Don't let that happen. Before your frustration reaches the point that you feel like you will become violent (I consider shouting as violent because it teaches the dog nothing but to fear

What do you do if the dog won't listen? Don't get angry; just snap on the leash and reinforce your training.

you.), stop your training session and take a break. That break may last as long as a day, but don't let the challenges inherent in teaching an animal push you to the point of doing something that will 1.) Be abusive to the animal; 2.) Reduce the effectiveness of your training session and 3.) Make you consider, even for a minute, that your dog can't be trained in basic obedience.

If you are like most dog owners, you will never enter a competition of any sort with your pet. But all of us want our dogs to come, sit and lie down on command. We don't want the dog barking all night long, and we would enjoy walking the dog much more if we weren't getting dragged all over town by a hyperactive canine. This book is not about creating a hunting dog, training an agility champion or teaching your family pet to track down missing fugitives, but you can bet all those dogs have mastered the basic skills that will be presented here.

Let's get back to the issue of patience. Like I said before, dogs don't think like you and me. And, to be honest, when it comes to training, I don't know that I care if a dog reasons at all. What I want is for the dog to react to the stimuli that I present. If I call, I want the dog to come, immediately. If I say "sit," I want the dog to sit and not get up until I call. These consistent reactions to my commands constitute what I call a well-trained dog. It is important to understand that you have a personal relationship with your dog, and the training you provide is only administered to suit your desires. To put it simply, you want the dog to do what you want the dog to do. If you want the dog to heel on your left side or your right side, who am I to say otherwise? The key to getting the dog to do what you want is patience. Combine that with a little bit of repetition, and your dog will respond to the training.

Training through repetition is where most people get tangled up believing, "I don't have time to train a dog." That statement is simply not true. You have the time because dogs have wonderful memories for routines. But sometimes, it just takes them a while to realize that what you are doing is establishing a routine. That's why you need to be patient, repetitive and consistent. If you lose your cool, especially if you do it repeatedly, all the dog is going to remember is, "That person yells a lot and hits me. I'm not going over there." On the other hand, if you give the same command and consistently demand the same reaction to that command, then praise the success and consistently correct the failures. Your dog will understand and will soon respond without hesitation.

Here's a prime example: Our loving dog owner takes Rover out to the park for some exercise. There aren't too many people or pets around, so he decides to let Rover off the leash for a little run. Rover runs. And runs. Soon our dog owner is calling and calling until he is red in the face. And Rover is still running. The anger builds in our loving dog owner. The calling (really shouting) continues and finally Rover is done running and trots back up to the boss. The dog owner is, by this time, not such a loving master any more. He is, in fact, furious. He grabs Rover's collar, shakes the dog, hollers some more and ends up giving the dog a good slap alongside the ear.

That dog owner has just taught his pet something. But it was the wrong thing. Rover heard his master calling, decided (finally) to respond and when he got there, he got yelled at, shaken and hit. Most people assume, especially when they are upset with a dog that won't

The lowest level of dominance behavior is simply a stern look. Think mean. Look tough.

"behave," that dogs somehow reason like people. It's faulty logic. Dogs don't reason. Rover doesn't know that he got hit because he failed to respond to the first command. Rover only knows that he got hit. In the dog's mind, the sequence of events described very likely registered like this: "He called me. I came. He hit me."

Do you think Rover is going to come right away the next time he's called? He certainly won't if the result is a slap to the ear. Would you?

You need to be firm, but not violent. One of the best ways to remember this is to always remind yourself that you got the dog as a companion. The dog is supposed to bring you happiness. If you find yourself getting stressed, stop and think about the dog as your companion. Then also remember that in most cases of "disobedience" the dog is just being a dog. The animal is simply acting on the instincts that make her a dog, and your training has not yet convinced the dog to ignore instinct when you issue a command.

Know Your Dog

Dogs, at the very core of their being, need to live in a pack. The pack mentality is woven so deeply into the inner workings of every dog that

Leaning over the top of a dog is the second level of establishing dominance. Most dogs will submit to this level.

Once you put your hand on a dog's shoulder, you are clearly telling the animal you mean business. If the dog moves away or throws a paw up at your hand, he is rejecting your claim of dominance.

there is no hope of trying to overcome it, change it or ignore it. Those of us who hope to train dogs have got to understand what the pack means to the dog and use that knowledge to help train the dog.

When canines first roamed the forests, the pack provided everything, from training and discipline to camaraderie and food. In this modern world, we've taken the dog from the woods, removed the animal from its system of communal living and, finally, we demand that she act in accordance with our rules and social norms. We are expecting a lot from our dogs. And we can best train them by providing some semblance of life in a pack. You must take the place of the pack.

The great thing about this is that your dog makes it easy. Your dog wants nothing more than to be with you. When you leave for the day, the dog, unless she is suffering from acute separation anxiety, simply lies down and waits for you to come back. When you come back, the dog is happy again because she knows she is part of the pack.

So now you've got to teach the dog its place in the pack. As the dog's trainer, you must assume the role of — to use the politically correct term — the alpha figure. All relationships in the pack are based on a social hierarchy. You are the leader. You make the rules. You issue the rewards. You provide the corrections when a member of your pack steps out of line. Once the dog understands that you are the leader, training comes very easily. This is because dogs in the pack very seldom challenge the leader once the hierarchy has been established. Sure, after several years a young wolf may step up to assume leadership of the pack once the alpha wolf starts to show his age but, for the most part, order is established through dominance. You need to be the dominant member of the pack in order to train your dog

The tricky part is to show the dog you are in charge without breaking the animal's spirit. This is not as difficult as it sounds. You've just got to communicate like a dog. Luckily, no barking is required. Almost all of the dominance indicators one dog shows to another are silent. Here they are in order from the least to most severe.

The Look

You know this look; it's the one your mother gave you as a child when you were acting up at a social gathering. That direct, piercing stare is powerful. It is especially powerful when used against dogs. It is a challenge. The look lets the dog know you are not happy with the animal's current behavior. Young dogs are especially intimidated by this type of activity and will often drop their head and assume a submissive posture immediately. That's when you both know you are in charge.

The Lean

Without saying a word, you can convince most dogs that you're the boss by simply moving in close and leaning over the dog. This is an even more direct challenge than staring at the dog. If I have a dog that won't sit, I'll never give the command a second time. I'll just move in close and look down at the dog. Presto—no more defiance of that command.

Grabbing the throat clearly lets the dog know you are the boss. This shouldn't be required often, but when it is, it is the only thing that works. If you accompany this with some growling, you'll feel the dog submit.

The Touch

It is very common in wolf packs for the dominant wolf to approach other wolves and place his muzzle or paws on the shoulder of a subordinate animal. When you praise your dog and pet the animal on the shoulder, you are doing the same thing. This is a great way to provide encouragement while at the same time show you are in command. Use this technique often and your training will be very easy.

Grabbing the Throat

This is the only dominance behavior that requires any noise to be made. If you have a dog that is particularly stubborn and refuses to accept your position as the leader of the pack, you've got to go for the throat. There is no intent here to harm the dog. You are simply communicating in a manner that the dog, through tens of thousands of years of evolution, will understand completely. Kneel down and let the dog come in close. Get one hand on the collar and pull the dog to the ground as you roll the animal to his back. Grab the throat (carefully but firmly) and shake the dog roughly while you growl loudly. As you let the dog up, lean over her and keep one hand firmly on the dog's shoulders. You should only have to do this a few times, and the animal will get the message.

Other important aspects of establishing and maintaining dominance include taking control, keeping control and giving commands.

Taking control means just that: You must immediately establish a leadership role with the dog. If you have a puppy, this is pretty easy. The dog is small, and you are big. You can simply pick up the dog if you have to, and there is no danger of the little critter yanking your arm out of joint when you attach the leash.

If you are dealing with a bigger and/or older dog, the issue of control takes on more importance. Untrained or under-trained adult dogs are generally accustomed to doing pretty much whatever they want. In most cases, these dogs are, at their core, good dogs. Watch an untrained dog — if it's your dog, stop being mad at the dog long enough to really look at what the dog is doing. You'll notice that the animal seems to romp and wander, flitting from one place to the next trying to encourage every person or animal she comes in contact with to play. An untrained dog simply does not know its place and does not understand that dogs are supposed to take orders from humans. Get the leash on such a dog and prepare for some tugging as you use some of the dominance tricks previously explained. The first step in getting control is to display dominance. You'll also find that training such a dog takes more repetition before the dog decides that what you command really is the thing to do. Just don't give up. Your job is to be more persistent than the dog.

Everything you do should reinforce to the dog that you are in control of the pack. When you bring out the dog's food, make the dog sit and wait to eat until you say it's OK to do so. When you open the door to take the dog out for a walk or a training session, make the dog wait so you can step outside first. In the wild, the dominant dog also decides when it's time to play and when the pack will get up and move

28

A correction is
nothing more
than a quick tug
that gets the
dog's attention.

Praise is a powerful
motivator for most
dogs. Canines
simply want to
please. Show a
dog he has done
something well and
he, will do it again.

to a new location. You need to fill all those roles to be an effective trainer. All of this is pack behavior, and you are constantly showing your dominance in subtle ways.

The Correction

Throughout this book you'll see the term "correction." Most of the time I'll use this term when I want you to apply a short, sharp tug on the leash to remind the dog you are in charge, and whatever the dog just did was not appropriate. A correction is quick and immediate. Never yank on the leash. Never lift the dog off the ground by the leash. Never whip the dog with the leash. Just give a short, sharp tug. If you need to add strength to the correction, say "no" in a firm voice as you give the correction. Combine that with staring at the dog or leaning over the animal, and you'll be amazed at how quickly a dog comes to figure out that if he does what is asked, no correction is needed.

Of course, there are always exceptions to the rule. If you really need to get a dog's attention, there are two additional levels of correction you can apply. The first is to grab the nape of the neck and lift the dog's forelegs off the ground as you look directly into the dog's eyes. The second should only be used in extreme cases. Grab the dog by the nape of the neck and the skin over the dog's hind legs and lift the whole animal off the ground about 3 inches, shake her a bit and say "no" quite firmly.

The thing to remember about a correction, regardless of the level of intensity, is that it must be immediate. A dog doesn't remember what he did 10 minutes ago. The sequence must be swift: infraction/correction. Then immediately continue training. Tugging the leash five times won't do any more good than tugging it once. If a tug doesn't work, add a look. Then add a lean. Then, finally, pick the dog up. He'll get the message.

The other side of the correction coin is praise. Use it often but make it meaningful.

Meaningful praise is applied just like a correction: immediately. As soon as the dog does something you like, smile and say "good dog." This is a great time, too, to rub the dog on the shoulders, explaining to the animal that the dominant member of the pack approves of the action.

When calling a dog to you, just say the dog's name and command "come." Keep it simple.

Praise can be anything from a simple expression to a syrupy and congratulatory "gooooood dog. What a good dog. Yeah. You did it. Yes. Goooood dog." All that really matters is that the dog knows you are happy, and you issue the praise as soon as the good behavior is completed. Remember, completed is the key word. If you are teaching the dog to come, provide the praise as soon as the dog arrives (sometimes it even helps to get excited while the dog is on her way to you). But, if you are teaching the dog to sit still for a long period of time, it only stands to reason that you should withhold the praise until the dog has sat as long as you wanted her to. If the dog gets up and moves before you give the command, it doesn't make any sense to praise the animal. You need to apply the praise at the right time and withholding praise can often be as effective a training tool as applying it.

Commands

I'll close this discussion with a brief primer on commands. I saved it for the end of the section so it will be fresh in your mind as you start training your dog. Commands are the verbal link between you and your dog. All the other non-verbal dominance behaviors, the use of the leash, praise and corrections are secondary to the commands you give your dog. Commands are so important that I've included another short chapter about how you use them. Right now I want to review the commands I suggest you use to train your dog. You may choose to use others but, if you do, please follow these guidelines. Commands should be:

- One syllable
- Given in a direct and clear voice
- Words that are not easily confused

Here are the basic ones we'll be using. I'll include a short explanation of what not to do when you give these commands only because, as simple as they seem, if you don't give commands correctly, your training will be all the more difficult.

Sit: This is it. One word. Short and to the point. Don't muck it up by adding anything else, especially the word "down."

Down: This is what you say when you want the dog on her belly. If you teach from this book, then forget these commands and later tell your dog "sit down," the animal will be confused and may not know how to respond.

Repetition and patience make for a great training combination, but keep the sessions short and end them on a positive note.

Come: This is the command everyone messes up. Don't be saying things like "C'mere. Here boy. Get here. Over here." Or anything else. Just say "come."

Heel: When you want the dog to walk at your side, give this command. Properly teaching a dog to heel does a lot of things. Most importantly, it teaches the dog to pay attention to you. When you move, the dog is to move. When you stop, the dog is to stop.

Quiet: Teaching a dog to remain silent can be a tough task. Depending on how you want to do it, you may end up using this command. Similar to "come," people sometimes, in anger, add some extra words. Don't. Your dog will learn more quickly if you keep it simple.

No: This is the universal command to keep your dog from doing anything you don't want her to do. Combine it with a show of dominance, and you get control quickly.

Fetch: Because this is every dog's favorite game, you'll want to work this into your training and playtime routines.

Naming Rights

While not technically a training issue, the name you choose for your dog can either assist or confuse the commands you hope to use. Do you remember the comedian who named his dog Sit? Don't do that. Better yet, go with a two-syllable name for your puppy. Names like Echo, Denver, Lucky and Brandy work very well with single-syllable commands. Say some of these out loud, and you'll notice how forceful the combination of a two-syllable name, followed by a one-syllable command can be. You realize, of course, the dog doesn't really understand English. She's waiting to hear a sound (in this case a word) that will prompt her to act. The word might mean something to us humans, but as far as the dog is concerned, you could train the animal to respond to any word in the world as long as you are consistent.

The name game is also important when giving commands, especially if you have more than one dog. I always encourage people to say the name of the dog first before giving the command. For example, "Echo, sit." Or "Buddy, come." Doing so teaches the dog to respond to her name and also gives her a chance to get ready for the upcoming command. When she hears her name, she [knows a] command is coming and can focus on you.

Owners with several dogs will find things much more [easier when] one dog responds to each command. Think about it. If y[ou had] dogs sitting in front of you when you throw a ball and say ["fetch," you] could end up with a melee on your hands. If, on the other hand, you say "Lucky, fetch," you can be reasonably sure only one dog is going to race after the ball.

As I said at the start, training dogs is not difficult and it doesn't really take a lot of time. What it does take is consistency, repetition and a little bit of patience. Dogs that are new to your home will test you. The older the dog is when you start the training, the more the dog will test you. The dog is not doing this with any sort of malice intended. The animal is just being a dog and trying to find its place in your pack. "Speak" to the dog on its own terms, in a language it can understand, and you will be heard. The best part is that success is easy to see. You know you're doing it right when both you and the dog are happy during and after the training session.

Older dogs will also require more persistence and patience during training. You've got to remember that with an older dog you are now doing remedial work. The dog already has learned many ways of doing things. You are trying to change those ways. There's bound to be some resistance, and it is sure to take a while before the dog understands that your "new" commands are part of her routine. I know I've said it before, but don't give up. Just be more patient and persistent than your dog. If you do so, your dog will get the message sooner than you think. Now let's get started. ✃

A good dog is a good dog, no matter the breed. All it takes is a little bit of consistency while you are training. Do it correctly and any dog can be a great dog.

Chapter 3

The Training Session

Training should be fun for both you and the dog. Keeping the sessions to 15 minutes means it won't become drudgery.

Each of the following chapters describes in detail what you'll be doing to train your dog, but one of the most important aspects of that training is how you organize it and where you conduct it. Putting a little forethought into your training sessions will insure that you get the most benefit and fun out of time you spend working with your dog.

Keep the Training Brief

Our goal here is to train by devoting 15 minutes each day. This type of training works because several short training sessions are better than one long one. You can even go a step farther by breaking your 15-minute sessions into five-minute segments with a minute or two of playtime tucked between each training session.

This all works because dogs, especially young or untrained dogs, have really short attention spans. The key to solid training in a short time is to get the dog's attention, reinforce simple commands quickly, then quit before the dog gets sick of you and tunes you out. After a short break for some play or a walk, you can get right back to the training while the last lesson is still fresh in the dog's head. By keeping the training segments short, your dog not only doesn't get bored, he also doesn't get physically tired, either. A dog that is fresh and alert takes to training better than one that just wants to lie down and rest.

Another argument for keeping the training sessions short is that you'll be more likely to maintain a regular schedule. Let's face it, we all have demands on our time. If you thought for a minute that you'd need two solid hours each day to train your dog, what would happen to your dog? But knowing that you only need 15 minutes makes it more likely that you'll get out there and train the dog. The sessions are short, the work is easy and you'll very likely begin to look at the outings as stress-relieving instead of stress-inducing. So, really, everybody wins when the training sessions are kept short.

Finally, there's no rule that says you only have to train your dog once a day. That's just the minimum you should shoot for. If you want to arrange for a pair of sessions, one in the morning and one at night, your training will go all the faster. And, the dog won't know the difference; he'll just like the fact that he's getting out and doing something. One of the keys to multiple training sessions on a single day is to strike the right balance between repetition and variety. If you run multiple sessions daily for a week or more, your dog might get bored with doing the same thing over and over. True, the repetition is the training tool, but you have to introduce at least a little bit of variety, too. It can be playtime with some surprise commands thrown in or can be switching from one command to something similar. For instance, you would do well to teach "sit" and "heel" during alternate morning and evening training sessions because one command builds on the skills of the other.

Picking a Spot

Training does not require a huge amount of space or tons of fancy equipment. In fact, I once met a rancher in South Dakota who trained a cattle dog to respond to its first whistle command while the two rode across the state in the man's pickup truck. The man wanted the dog to lie down in response to one short blast of the whistle. After seven hours in the truck, the dog knew how.

This is an extreme example, but it does present a lot of good information. The training area, in this case the front seat of the

Good training doesn't have to take a long time. But it does require your dog's undivided attention.

pickup truck, was confined. This meant the dog couldn't get away. There were also very few distractions, meaning the dog had to focus on the trainer. Like I said, this training in a truck is an extreme example, but it does provide the combination you want, especially for early training. Once the dog is responding adequately to your commands in a controlled setting, you can allow a few distractions. But start your training where you have complete control and your dog's undivided attention.

Most dog owners will do really well working with the dog in a backyard. The dog doesn't really need to be fenced in because you'll be doing all of your early training with the aid of a leash. But, if there is a fence, that's all the better.

Lacking a backyard, dog owners might need to be a bit more creative. Apartment dwellers can work with small dogs right in the hallway, though you may want to go easy on the whistle commands. If there is a quiet corner available at a city park, by all means put it to good use. Vacant lots, school playgrounds (when not in use), parking lots (during the early morning hours) and community green spaces all work well as training locations. The idea is that you find a place where the dog can feel comfortable and concentrate on the training.

Establishing a Schedule

Dogs, like many people, are creatures of habit. When it comes right down to it, we are really just teaching the dog to get into the habit of obeying our commands. This will happen much more quickly if the dog isn't surprised by something new and different each time you snap on the leash. There will be a time when it's important to change the location and the look of the training but, initially, you'll want to go to the same place at the same time. This routine will also help you to stick to your training schedule. The dog will quickly become comfortable and confident at your training location. This allows the animal to focus on your commands and instructions. Once your dog responds to every command while in the controlled setting, it's time to move on to some place with a few more distractions. Remember, everything is a stepping-stone. You are building on each previous success in order to move up the training ladder.

One side benefit of sticking to a training schedule is that the schedule will also help with the housebreaking of your dog. Scheduling is one of the key elements in training when and where to do "his business." This is yet another situation where the elements of training not only build on each other, but also are so entwined that you most certainly will find yourself teaching several important things at once. Unless you pay really close attention, you may not even know you're doing such a good job training your dog.

As you read through this book, you'll come to find that each training session can and should be used to teach new skills and reinforce those things you've already worked on. Each outing serves to build on the training of the last session. And, if you are consistent with your commands, every walk to the curb, every trip to the park and every picnic at the lake becomes an additional training experience for the dog. Follow a schedule, do things consistently and before long your dog will be on autopilot. You can benefit from a training session just about anywhere you go. But, if you adhere to a schedule, especially during your early training, the dog will quickly come to know what is expected. And that's exactly what you want. 🦴

Chapter 4

Where Training Begins

38

Teaching your dog to sit is the foundation upon which you will build total control. This is where everything starts. The other basic obedience commands, even "heel," will be taught, and very often given, when the dog is sitting. "Sit" should be thought of as your most powerful command. You should train for it in such a manner that your dog will respond instantly, no matter the circumstances, when you command "sit." For that reason, it's important to not only teach this command thoroughly but also to reinforce it throughout the rest of your training session.

Where Training Begins

Teaching your dog to sit is the foundation upon which you will build total control. This is where everything starts. The other basic obedience commands, even "heel," will be taught, and very often given, when the dog is sitting. "Sit" should be thought of as your most powerful command, and you should train for it in such a manner that your dog will respond instantly, no matter the circumstances, when you command "sit." For that reason, it's important to not only teach this command thoroughly but also to reinforce it throughout the rest of your training session. Teaching your dog to sit is the foundation upon which you will build total control. This is where everything starts. The other basic obedience commands, even "heel," will be taught, and very often given, when the dog is sitting. "Sit" should be thought of as your most powerful command, and you should train for

Your goal: To have the dog sit instantly when you give the command by voice or whistle.
What you'll need: A leash, a whistle and some patience.

Having a dog that sits on command is a great feeling. Start training with the leash and you'll have no trouble at all.

it in such a manner that your dog will respond instantly, no matter the circumstances, when you command "sit." For that reason, it's important to not only teach this command thoroughly but also to reinforce it throughout the rest of your training session.

When you have a dog that sits on command, regardless of the distractions going on all around, you can be fairly confident that you won't have a lot of other problems, especially those associated with an over-exuberant animal. There will be no jumping up, no racing around the yard or the park, no pushing hard against your legs in an effort to get even more of your undivided attention. When the dog has been taught to sit, all you have to do is give the command, either

As soon as you give the command, push down on the dog's butt.

40

Using the leash and pushing on the dog's butt, puts the animal in position quickly.

by voice or with your whistle, and the dog stops whatever he is doing and sits. If you teach your dog nothing else in the world, requiring the animal to master this one simple command will give you control of your dog.

Right now you're likely saying, "Sure, that sounds great. How do I do it?" If you want your dog to drop his butt to the ground instantly every time you issue the command, let's start by reviewing your part.

Every dog will break early in the training. It's nothing to worry about. Just give a correction and put the dog back on his spot.

It pays to wait a while before you praise your dog. This teaches the dog to stay sitting until you give a release command.

- The voice command is "sit," and the corresponding whistle command is a single, short blast on the whistle.
- Training must begin on the leash, especially for older dogs. Puppies can come off the leash fairly soon, but older dogs will need weeks of repetition.
- Give the command once, then reinforce it by showing the dog exactly what you expect. Do not repeat the command.

As I previously mentioned, start with the leash securely clipped to the dog's collar. Now start walking. This will get the dog on its feet and provide a bit of initial distraction that the dog must overcome. After a few steps stop, give one blast on your whistle and say "sit." Then, while holding the leash tightly, gently but firmly push down on the dog's butt, directing the animal to the sitting position. As soon as the dog's hindquarters hit the ground, pet him on the head and offer lots of praise.

A hand in front of the face is a visual reminder that the dog is supposed to stay put.

This type of training actually teaches two things at once. By using the leash and taking a few steps before giving the command, the dog is also learning to sit at your side each time you stop walking; this is very nice when you are out for a stroll. But let's get back to the original lesson.

You've commanded "sit" and guided the dog to the sitting position. Now you praise him. With young or untrained older dogs, this praise will be enough to cause the dog to break from the sitting position. That's fine. Don't get upset. This is all part of the training. As soon as the dog breaks, give a short tug on the leash (this is your correction) and, if you need to, push down on the dog's butt to return the animal to the sitting position. Now, stand still and count silently to five or 10 before praising the dog. If the dog moves before you are done counting, do not repeat the command, but do repeat the correction. By doing this you are teaching the dog to sit until you say it's time to move again.

After you've counted to five or 10, praise the dog lavishly and repeat the process. Your goal is to slowly increase the amount of time you require your dog to sit in one place before you offer praise.

As you put some distance between you and the dog, a traditional correction becomes difficult. That's why it pays to reinforce early training while beside the dog. If that's done effectively, you may not have to give a correction from a distance.

During the first day of training, you might issue the command a dozen times, each time counting to 10. The next day, go through the same sequence but count to 20. In most cases, you'll be able to quit pushing down on the dog's butt after about the third day. By that time, the dog understands what "sit" means and is now just waiting for the praise and your permission to once again move about.

At this point, both you and your pet are learning about patience. It is difficult to imagine anything more boring than standing beside a dog that's trained well enough to sit still for several minutes. But you have to do it to keep the dog from moving until you say it's time to move. I think the longest I've gone, using my wristwatch as a timer, is five minutes. It seems like an eternity, but I figure that if dog will sit still for five full minutes, it's time to move on to the next phase of training.

Once you get to the end of your leash, you'll need to go with a longer check cord for more advanced training.

The 'Surprise' Command

I can't stress enough that teaching your dog to sit on command will be the foundation on which everything else is built. Practice daily until it is mastered (you'll be surprised how quickly a dog will catch on), but also include some playtime. At the end of each session, wrestle around on the ground with the dog or toss a retrieval dummy or a flying disc a few feet away and let the dog get used to picking it up. The dog needs this kind of fun and affection after a training session. It helps build the bond between you and the dog. It also gives you the opportunity to sneak in some very important training while you play.

It's called training with (or through) distractions. After you've finished with the bread and butter of your "real" training session and you've decided to spend a little bit of playtime with the dog, go ahead and get rough. Keep the dog on the leash, but play around. Chase the dog. Let him chase you. Wrestle a bit. Roll toys around. Do whatever it is you and your dog do for fun. Then, just as the dog's really getting into it—really having a great time—spring a good firm "sit" command on her.

To encourage compliance with this sort of snap command, make sure that you stop moving around as soon as you issue the command. It's not really fair to expect a dog in the early stages of training to sit still while you're still running around playing games. That's just too much distraction at this stage of the training. The goal of this type of snap command is to remind the dog that "sit" (like all other basic commands) is an absolute command that must be obeyed without hesitation each time it is given. By giving the command during playtime, you are reinforcing to the dog the idea that you set the schedule, make the decisions and give the orders. This is done with the leash still attached to the dog's collar so you can get control quickly if you need to and administer a correction if the dog fails to respond.

The sequence for praising the dog following a "snap" command is just the same as before. At first you can praise right away if you want to, but by this time, your dog will likely understand that "sit" means she is not to move until you say so. If that's the case and you can spring a snap "sit" command and your dog remains rock steady for five minutes or more, you can go on to additional training. The next phase is being able to give the command from a distance. This is the

Hiding around a corner is advanced stuff. Start with the dog on a check cord, but soon you'll be able the work with the dog off the leash.

really cool stuff. When you can command your dog to sit, even if the animal is a block away, all your neighbors will look at you with awe and wonder at how you've learned to work such magic. The best part is that it's so simple; anyone can do it.

After your dog sits for as long as you can put up with standing by her side, try backing away. Initially, you won't be backing away too far. The first step here is to move from the side of the dog to directly in front of it. At this time, you'll still be holding the leash.

The average dog will think you are starting to walk again and move to go with you. Give a bit of a correction and hold your hand, palm

To really teach sitting at a distance, you've got to have a long cord and patience. Just keep at it.

This is what you want. A well-trained dog will sit, with or without the leash, when you give the command.

facing the dog, directly in front of the dog's nose. You are teaching the dog that the "sit" command must be obeyed, even if the master moves. So, start by giving the command. Once the dog is sitting, step in front of her. Correct and reinforce with the leash and your hand as needed. When the dog remains still for a 10-count, take a step back. Count again and take another step back.

If you haven't figured it out by now, you'll quickly notice that you are putting enough distance between you and the dog to make the typical correction with the leash difficult or even impossible.

Chapter 5

Teaching the Dog to Come

Dogs should always enjoy coming to their owners. But they should also come on command without any delay.

48

So, now that your dog will stay sitting while you walk into the house for a glass of tea, what's next?

Having a dog that will come when it's called is always nice. It's more than nice; it is a requirement. If you don't want to be chasing your dog all over town, or sitting on the front porch waiting for him to return; if you want to be able control your dog at a distance to keep her away from dangerous situations; if you want to prove to the neighbors that they have nothing to fear when you let your dog go for a run, then your dog needs to come when called. And again, the dog should respond the first time you call and come every time. There can be nothing more important to your dog than responding to your command to come.

That, of course, leads us to the same old question, "How do we get there?" Once again I'll tell you. We don't get there; we start there.

Your goal:
To get the dog headed your way immediately when called by voice or whistle.

What you'll need:
A long check cord, a whistle and some dog treats.

Because the dog now knows how to sit, teaching her to come is easy. Just call and pull on the check cord.

Back when I was trying to train my very first dog, I watched a video that showed a dog sitting in a field and running to his master's side after a single blast on the whistle. The announcer went on to say, "This seemingly simple task requires the training of no less than 12 different commands and takes months to master." My first thought was, "It can't be that hard." I was right. It's not really that hard at all.

While there may be tons of subtle nuances you can introduce and describe as training steps for calling a dog, when it comes right down to it, teaching a dog to come is just about the easiest thing in the world once you've trained the animal to sit. Get yourself about 25 feet of rope and attach a snap loop on the end. Hook it to the dog's collar. Command the dog to sit and then back away about 10 feet. Kneel down. Give several quick blasts on the whistle, say the dog's name, and then say "come." That should start the animal moving in your direction. If the dog deviates, pull on the rope just like you are reeling in a fish and say "come." When the dog arrives, lavish the animal with praise. Then, command the dog to sit before backing up a bit farther and trying it again.

You'll notice that I use a whistle right from the beginning when teaching a dog to come. You'll find out early on that whistles carry much better than your voice. A whistle can be heard above the din of road noise, over the voices of children playing in the parks and across

Bend over and welcome the dog. Get her excited about coming to your side.

There's no reason to delay issuing praise when a dog comes as called. The dog responded correctly and ample praise will insure she does it next time, too.

all but the biggest ponds. With the exception of blowing a whistle during a stiff headwind, you can believe that your dog has heard the whistle command. If the dog doesn't come when you blow it, he may be choosing to ignore you. This means you've got some more training to do with the long cord.

So, let's go back to a discussion of the early training for "come." You want to make yourself as inviting as possible when teaching the dog to come. The goal is to make the dog happy to see you and happy to be by your side. I've heard all sorts of advice on using treats as a reward

Several short blasts on the whistle, usually three to five, should follow your voice command. The blasts will certainly get your dog's attention.

A stout collar and a good check cord will get the dog moving in your direction.

for a proper response. You call. The dog comes. You provide a little biscuit or snack. Some trainers say it's the only way to teach a dog to come, others have told me, "When you're out of treats, you're out of luck." Well, then maybe just plan ahead and don't run out of treats. The flipside of that discussion is that praise should usually be effective enough as a reward to get a dog to come to you. If you are down there at dog-level, talking in a happy voice, 99 percent of all dogs will come to you, especially if you are pulling on the rope to provide a little bit of guidance. But then again, a biscuit couldn't hurt.

You can probably see that I have no really strong feelings on what you should do to get a dog to come to you. But I do have very strong feelings on what you shouldn't do.

If you call and the dog doesn't respond immediately, start pulling on the check cord.

Never call the dog in an angry voice. Never, ever, ever hit the animal when it arrives. To do so is punishing the dog for doing what you asked, and before long no dog with any sense at all will come to you when you call if the result is a beating. This bears repeating, and I don't think I can stress it enough. Dogs know when you are angry. Yet, no matter how far off the dog runs, what it has done while it was away or how frustrated you are by the animal's continued desire to romp about without listening to a word you are saying, never, never punish a dog for coming to you. To do so is not only cruel, but will also totally disrupt any training you are trying to accomplish.

Also, pay close attention to the command you are giving. The command is "come." It is not "come 'ere, here boy, get here, come on" or anything else you might decide to say. For consistency's sake, the command should also be preceded by several short blasts on the whistle. This is especially important early in the training when you are encouraging the dog to respond to both your voice and the whistle. As the training progresses a little bit, you can call just by voice or just with the whistle. Indeed, you should mix in a couple of each of these commands during each training session. This is to let your dog know that regardless of which command (voice or whistle), she should respond immediately.

Now, if you're starting with a dog you've rescued from the local animal shelter or have an older dog that never really got the idea that "come" means just that, your on-leash training will run a little longer than training a puppy to respond to the same command. Don't get frustrated. As before, this is just a matter of teaching the dog the new rules. You use the rope to reinforce the fact that when you call, the dog can do nothing other than come to you. This is not a game. It is not playtime. This is serious business, and there can only be one proper response when you call. With older dogs or refugees from the animal shelter, it's all the more important that you create a happy atmosphere surrounding the issuance of the command. But let there be no confusion between you and the dog, it still is a command. You issue it. The dog obeys it. No discussion.

Those last three little sentences work very well for younger dogs. But, as always, those "problem cases" require continued patience and several weeks of repetitive training on the leash before you can even think about releasing the line and hoping the dog will respond

As you advance through each step of the training, you are building on the previous lessons. Here, the dog is sitting at a distance...

... and coming on command. She's coming so quickly she had to turn a bit to avoid running into my legs.

appropriately when you call. Untrained or under-trained dogs have a wonderful memory for what it's like to be free from the confines of things like commands and leashes. I once worked daily for six weeks with an untrained 3-year-old German shorthair pointer. The dog was kept on the leash for the entire time. At the end of 42 days, the dog responded like a show champion to every command I gave. On day 43 I decided to remove the leash and see what happened without the tether. I unhooked the leash and before the snap hit the ground that dog had shifted into warp drive. Three hours later a muddy, tired-looking pointer showed up at my front door, and I snapped on the leash and continued the on-leash work for another four weeks.

A good rule of thumb is to train on the leash until you think the dog has the command mastered, then train for two more weeks before opening the snap. Even then, keep off-leash training sessions short and keep the dog close by until you are sure every command you give will be followed.

Some dogs just seem to know the difference between being on the leash and being free of it. When you find a dog that smart, you've got to be very careful about how you conduct your off-leash training. Often it becomes a matter of starting almost at the beginning of your training cycle, except now you've removed the leash. That's to say that after the dog responds perfectly, even from extended distances on the leash, you've got to start over by keeping the animal very close to you as you first let go of the leash.

You read that correctly. Don't unhook the leash. Just let go of it. That way you have what amounts to an extended handle if the dog tries to get away. And, if you plant your foot firmly on the leash that your dog is dragging away, he administers his own instant correction.

Combining Lessons

Just because you are now teaching the dog to come, does not mean that you should abandon work on the "sit" command. On the contrary, now is the perfect time to combine some of the lessons to really reinforce the building block philosophy of training.

After your dog is coming to you reasonably well on the long leash (which may even be the first day of training), it's time to spring a surprise command just to make sure the dog is paying attention. Give the command "sit" and back away. After a few seconds, call the dog. When the animal is halfway to you, step forward, hold out one hand and say "sit." The dog will, at first, be a bit confused. After all, you just called, and now you are changing your mind. The best part is, it's your right. You can change your mind any time you want, and the dog must listen.

Anyway, chances are your dog will not stop right away the first time you try this. If the dog keeps coming after you command "sit," take a few more steps forward and give the dog a good stern look in the eye. You might want to add the word "no" at this time, but the object is to do as little talking as possible. If the dog stops but does not sit, approach and push down on the butt while pulling up on the leash. When the dog is sitting, provide lots of praise while you rub on the shoulders. Then command "sit" and back away again to start the process over.

Some professional trainers use a gadget called a "whoa pole" for this type of training. It's really nothing more than a post in the ground with a ring attached firmly to it. The long leash (in this case a really long line) is run through the loop and attached to the collar. The dog is commanded to sit, and the handler backs away, holding the bitter end of the line. When the dog is called, the trainer lets the line flow until it is time to command the dog to sit. The command is issued, and the trainer grabs the line and hangs on, jerking the dog to a stop. Gloves are advised for this training.

This type of training goes a bit beyond basic, but it is sometimes required for really stubborn dogs.

It's important to mix up the sequence, sometimes letting the dog come all the way to you while at other times ordering her to stop. The goal is to remind her that you are in control, and the last command is always the one to listen to, even if it is the direct opposite of one given before it. So, mix things up a little bit. As we continue to add more commands to the training sessions, the opportunity to build on the lessons of the past increases geometrically. This keeps things interesting for both you and the dog and insures that past training is not forgotten, even as new lessons are incorporated.

So, remember the goal. You want the dog to come the first time you call. To achieve this, use the long line well after you think you don't need it anymore. Training like this, 15 minutes at a time, three to five times a week, will really put you on the road to creating a great dog.

Chapter 6

Getting Down

A dog that will lie down and wait for you to give the next command is the very model of an "easy keeper." Master this training sequence and you'll have very little to worry about.

57

When you want your dog to lie down, nothing else will really do. It's important to understand that when you command your dog "down," it's really like an extension of the command "sit." Both commands do about the same thing since they require the dog to remain in one place until you command otherwise. "Down" offers the added benefit of reinforcing your dominance. In short, when you make a dog lie down, it's a lot like you are putting your hands on his shoulders. Remember that from a previous chapter? A dog that is down is agreeing to assume a submissive posture. That alone may be enough to make training this command a bit more difficult with some strong-willed dogs. With an older, untrained or under-trained dog, teaching "down" can be downright frustrating. But don't give up.

"Down" is a great command for extended rests. If you're sitting in a park reading, watching the kids' Little League game or anywhere you'll be in one spot for a while,

Your goal: To teach the dog to drop to its belly every time you command "down."

What you'll need: A leash and a dog.

The first step is to have the dog sit, then drop a little slack in the leash.

Put your foot in the loop and give the command, "down."

give the "down" command. And, if your training has gone well, you can just about forget about the dog for a while. One more reason to teach the command well is that it provides another level of control in several situations, not the least important is when visitors (especially new visitors) drop by your home or apartment. Life is so much easier when you can simply give the dog a one-word command. Teach "down" well and you'll never again find yourself grabbing and overly excited dog by the collar and dragging her off to the porch or the bedroom as you tell your guest, "Wow, she really likes you."

Step down on the leash and guide the dog to the ground.

If the dog breaks, give a correction and push on the shoulders to get the dog back to the ground.

I'll start out with a reminder here. The command is "down." Forget about all those other things you might be tempted to say. Be simple. Be direct and be consistent. Doing so will make the training easier on both you and the dog – not that this operation is all that difficult to accomplish in the first place.

Adjust the dog's posture to reinforce good habits.

Here's what you'll do. To teach the dog to get on her belly, you'll need to have control of the animal. As previously mentioned, getting a dog to lie down on command is an act of dominance. If a dog wants to lie down on her own, well, that's another story. But when you make a dog lie down, it's a clear sign that you are in charge. To that end, you'll need to start with the dog on the leash.

Clip on the leash and walk slowly around your training area. If you've recently been working on "heel," your dog will likely sit every time you stop. That's fine. In fact, that's great because a sitting dog is halfway to down. When you stop walking, command "sit" and allow the dog to comply. Once the dog is sitting, command "down" and immediately step down on the slack part of the leash close to the dog's collar. The downward pressure pushes the animal's forequarters to the turf with very little effort on your part. Issue praise immediately.

Ideally, you want the dog down but in an erect posture. Think of the Sphinx. That's a beautiful posture for a dog in the down position.

The rest of the training should progress pretty much like teaching the dog to sit. Once you've commanded "down" and guided the dog to her belly, you can praise her. If your dog has mastered the "sit" command, you should have no trouble with the dog breaking, that is, moving from the down position. Just for the sake of training, or, if you've decided to teach "down" before you teach "sit", let's assume the dog breaks. Just like I said in the chapter on teaching the dog to sit, don't get upset. Breaking is part of the training. It happens. You just train through it.

As soon as the dog breaks, give a short tug on the leash (this is your correction) and, if you need to, push down on the dog's shoulders to return the animal to the "down" position. Now, stand still and count silently to five or 10 before praising the dog. If the dog moves before you are done counting, do not repeat the command but repeat the correction. By doing this, you are teaching the dog to stay down until you say it's time to move again.

After you've counted to five or 10, praise the dog lavishly and repeat the process. Your goal is to slowly increase the amount of time you require your dog to lie in one place before you offer praise. During the first day of training, you might issue the command a half a dozen times, each time counting to 10. If you've taught the dog to sit, you may have no trouble at all. The next day, go through the same

Don't let the dog get away with breaking. Approach the animal and gently but firmly push her back into position.

sequence but count to 20. In most cases, you'll be able to quit pushing down on the dog's shoulders in very short order. Three days, tops. By that time, the dog understands what "down" means and is waiting for the praise, and your permission to once again move around.

I'm repeating myself from the chapter on sitting, but once again, both you and your pet are learning about patience. It is difficult to imagine anything more boring than standing beside a dog that's trained well enough to lie still for several minutes. But you have to do it. Five minutes may seem like an eternity, but I figure that if a dog will lie still for five full minutes, it's time to move on to the next phase of training.

The 'Surprise' Command

Once the dog will go down and remain steady, it's time to include some playtime. Get wild, wrestle around on the ground with the dog or toss a ball or flying disc a few feet away and let the dog get used to picking it up. You did this while teaching the dog to sit, and it will work just as well with "down." Now you are going to sneak in some very important training while you play.

Your dog needs to work through distractions. After you've finished the "real" training session and you've decided to spend a little bit of playtime, do whatever it is you and your dog do for fun. Then, just as the dog's really getting into it, spring a good firm "down" command on her.

Again, I'm repeating myself here, but repetition is the key to good training. To encourage compliance with this sort of snap command, make sure that you stop moving around as soon as you issue the command. The goal of this type of snap command is to remind the dog that "down" (like all other commands) is an absolute command that must be obeyed without hesitation each time it is given. By giving the command during playtime, you are reinforcing on the dog the idea that you set the schedule, make the decisions and give the orders. This is done with the leash still attached to the dog's collar so you can get control quickly if you need to and administer a correction if the dog fails to respond.

The sequence for praising the dog following a "snap" command is

Distance training works best when the dog knows exactly what is expected when the command is given.

just the same as before. At first you can praise right away if you want to, but, by this time your dog will likely understand that "down" means he is not to move until you say so. The dog is simply there looking at you, not moving, waiting for the praise to come. A well-trained dog will wait all day for that praise. If that's the case and you can spring a snap command, and your dog remains rock steady for five minutes or more, you can go on to additional training.

But wait. Before you do that, you'll also want to make minor adjustments to the dog's posture. You don't want the animal rolling over on his side, or, worse yet, on his back. If the dog tends to do this, that's a sure sign the animal is feeling a little too submissive. To correct the problem, you simply correct the problem. That is to say, kneel down and physically, but calmly and gently, put the dog into the position you want. At this time, you can repeat the command, once. You'll say "down" as you do this, just to let the dog know what you expect after the command. The dog has to know what it is you want before it will remember the training sessions.

Distance Learning

The next phase is being able to give the command from a distance. This is the really cool stuff. When you can command your dog to sit, even if the animal is a block away, all your neighbors will look at you with awe and wonder at how you've learned to work such magic. The best part is it's so simple that anyone can do it.

After your dog stays down for as long as you can put up with standing by his side, try backing away. Just like in the chapter on sitting, you initially will not be backing away too far. The first step here is to move from the side of the dog to directly in front of him. Then back up two steps. At this time you'll still be holding the leash.

Next, call the dog to you, command him to sit and offer some praise. Then back up to the end of your leash. If your dog learned the sit command, this should be no trouble. Now command "down" and give the dog a few seconds to respond. If there is no movement, approach the dog and gently but firmly push down on the shoulders. Then back up to the end of the leash. Count to five and offer praise.

A correction at any distance is a bit tough. That is why I stress close control for the early stages of the distance "down" as well as the "sit" command. At close range you can administer a correction quickly and get the dog to comply promptly. One trick is to back up the length of your short leash and, as you issue the "down" command, bend at the knees and point to the ground. This usually gets the dog moving in the right direction. Some might call it cheating, but, if it works, I consider it a good option.

A command is just that. Even from a distance your dog should respond to every command.

Praise for the distance "down" is another key to getting a decent response. If, at a distance of about 6 feet (the length of your short leash) your dog drops to her belly on command, pause for a moment before you offer the praise. Then, praise lavishly. Give treats if you want to, but, by all means, let the dog know you are happy. If the dog does not drop immediately, offer no praise. By this point in the training, your dog should be conditioned to the fact that the proper response to a command earns praise. If the dog fails to respond as ordered, there is no happy talk, no treats, nothing. All that should happen is that you walk up and put the dog in the down position.

As with teaching "sit" from a distance, the idea here is to each day increase the distance from which you give the command, and the time the dog is required to remain down. You want the dog to understand that even if you are far away, "down" means just that.

As this training continues, your leash will become too short. Your long check cord may become too short, too. Don't worry. For this type of training, the cord is not really used for much of anything other than a reminder that you are in control. You can't use the check cord, or even a leash for that matter, to force a dog down from a distance. You've got to walk over there and force the issue from close range.

This is usually the time dog owners find out how much their dogs really love them. It happens like this: The dog is down at a distance and has actually dropped quickly to the command, leading you to believe everything is great. But, before too long, the dog starts to creep forward in an effort to be closer to you. It's actually rather comical to see a dog trying to low-crawl "unnoticed" in the direction of his best buddy. As funny as it looks, you should nip this in the bud right away.

The average person will say "stay." Let me remind you again about the command, actually the pseudo-command "stay."

If you teach "down" effectively, you shouldn't have to take the time to teach the dog another command to keep it in place. As with "sit," "down" means no movement is allowed until a release command is given. Of course, the dog will stay. Don't waste your breath and confuse the dog with a command that is not required.

The best thing you can do when a dog is trying to creep from the down position is to provide a good, firm "no." Combine that with a menacing stare and some more of the good power-posture stuff, and your dog will stop creeping in short order.

"Down" is a great command and a great place to be in your training. A dog that has mastered all the basic commands is a pleasure to be around. Once you get to this point, you've got very few worries and your frustration factor, as it relates to how your dog responds to commands, should be very low.

Chapter 7

Good Manners on the Line

Having a dog with good manners on the leash is more than just pleasant; it's safer and less frustrating.

Who wants to walk the dog? If that question gets nothing but groans of displeasure around your house, this chapter is for you. Every dog needs to have good manners, both on the leash and off. But teaching a dog to properly heel will make your life as a dog owner infinitely less frustrating and will very likely improve your attitude about walking the dog. And that says nothing about how much more fun the dog will have during your walks.

Before we really get into teaching the dog to heel, a short discussion about the leash is in order. Up to this point, the leash served only as a restraint; the word I like to use is "handle." It's something you grab onto to hold the dog, guide the dog to the

Your goal:
To keep your arm in its socket when you head out for a walk.
What you'll need:
A leash and a whistle.

A 6-foot leash is perfect for walks and general training work. Get one that's the right size for the dog. That is, don't make a little dog drag a big leash and don't expect to control a big dog with something too small.

Snaps should be simple and stout. This is one of many styles that will work fine.

sitting position or pull the dog to you when teaching him to come. Now, when you are teaching the dog to heel, there are some subtleties about the leash you should consider. First and foremost is to match the size of the leash to the size of the dog. You don't need 10 feet of half-inch rope to control a 10-week-old puppy. On the other hand, you also don't want a 60-pound Husky yanking you around as you try to get a grip on a tiny piece of nylon webbing.

Getting the dog moving is the easy part; just start walking.

If the dog begins to stray from your side, give a quick tug as a correction.

When you stop walking immediately command the dog to sit. If you do this regularly, the dog will sit without a word every time you stop.

For general training to heel and for most walks, a 6-foot leash is just fine if you match the weight of the material to the size of the dog. Get a good commercially made leash. You can make up your own long check cord for other training, but for your everyday leash, contact one of the retailers listed in the back of the book and order a good quality leash. Make sure the snap is stout but easy to use and always think about how the material feels in your hand.

Now we are ready to go. Through your work with earlier commands, your dog should understand by now what the leash is and how it will be used. The key to this exercise is to get the dog to concentrate on you and react to your movements when you issue the command.

Teaching these lessons is the same for all dogs. We start again with the leash clipped to the dog's collar. Give the command "sit" and stand beside the dog for a few seconds. If the dog still hasn't mastered sitting, stand for up to a minute. Then, without warning, start walking.

As soon as you move your first foot, say "heel" and give a gentle tug to get the dog going. Now that you're both moving, pay attention to the dog. What you are after is a dog that walks between 12 inches and 36 inches from your side and just about even with you. I've always allowed my dog to be about a pace ahead when I say heel, just so I can see the animal. You decide what you're comfortable with and be consistent. Don't allow the dog to run to the end of the leash one day and then require the animal to brush up against your knee the next. You'll confuse the dog.

The same goes for the side on which you choose to have your dog heel. To me, it only matters that you are comfortable with your choice and consistent in training. For the record, most hunting-dog trainers put their dogs on the left. That's because they usually carry a shotgun in their right hand while hunting. But if you want your dog on the right, fine. Remember, this is not about field trial and competition. This is about getting your dog to work the way you want it to. Just be consistent.

The most important thing you can do is be consistent. Don't let the dog get away with anything you don't want to put up with every time you take a walk.

Keep the dog on a leash until you are sure the animal understands and will obey the command to heel.

If the dog rushes ahead to the end of the leash, gather up about a foot of slack and give the leash a sharp jerk while simultaneously issuing the "heel" command quite firmly. Don't shout, but be firm.

At this stage in the training, take about 10 steps forward, then turn away from the dog, give a moderate tug on the leash and say "heel." The idea is to make the dog pay attention to what you are doing. At first you'll be pretty much walking in a big square, but you can do some things to add a bit of variety. Change your pace. Walk quickly. Jog if you like. Then, creep along slowly as if you are sneaking up on something. All the while keep a firm grip on the leash and make corrections, if needed, as described above. After a few sessions of always turning the same way, change directions. You will find your dog expecting you to turn the other way, and your knee will bump the dog's shoulder as you turn into him. No problem, just nudge the dog out of the way like you know where you're going. Soon the dog will begin to pay very close attention to you and react instantly as you change directions, start or stop walking. This is exactly what you want. When you command the dog to heel, she should be focused totally on what you are doing. She should be your little canine shadow. One of the best ways to encourage this is to make frequent turns as you are walking the dog. By doing so, you'll either bump the dog or tug on the leash and, either way, you'll be focusing the animal's attention on your actions. Soon it will become second nature to the dog to focus only on you.

When you stop walking, immediately command the dog to sit. This will teach her that her place is by your side. Reinforce this and your dog will understand that she must stay until you say it's fine to leave. The reinforcement also helps in your dog's training while you invest no extra time. During a single 15-minute lesson of teaching the dog to heel, you'll also be reinforcing the "sit" command and teaching the dog to sit every time you stop. This is where the training really starts to multiply. The dog is learning lots of things, and you are teaching more than you ever thought you could in such a short period. And, best of all, neither of you really notice how much is being done.

Use Caution

Here's a word of warning about starting to work the dog without the leash. You've read it before. Don't jump right into such activities for any training, especially "heel" and "come." Dogs learn by repetition. For you to consistently repeat your training sequence, you must have control of the dog through a leash. Once the dog follows each of the basic commands flawlessly while on the leash, keep it on for

This is the proper grip on the leash for training a dog to heel. Corrections are quick and easy when you maintain this grip.

Off-leash training starts with the dog dragging the leash. This way, you can apply an instant correction just by stepping on the leash.

Here's the instant correction in action. The dog got a bit too far in front, and the trainer simply stepped on the leash.

another week or two, and then think about unclipping the animal for advanced work.

Oh Yeah, the Advanced Work!

As simple as it is to get a dog to heel, it is also equally simple to let the dog slip back into bad habits. That, in turn, draws you into bad habits. You see, as the dog creeps farther and farther away after you've commanded him to heel, you end up issuing the command again and again; thus, teaching the dog to ignore the first command and only listen after you've talked yourself blue in the face.

To keep this from happening, use the leash often. Use the leash when you don't think you'll need it. Use it after you're sure that your dog has mastered the command. Use it occasionally without rhyme or reason and always issue corrections without words. A short, sharp tug will say more than you ever can.

As with all training, praise is very important when teaching a dog to heel. Training should be a happy time for dog and trainer.

So, now that you've got the dog accustomed to the idea that once you command "heel," he should go everywhere you go without as much assistance from the leash. A week or so after most dogs start to really understand what "heel" means, you can then drop the leash on the ground, letting the dog drag it alongside you. If the dog starts to move too far ahead of you or off to one side, just step down on the leash. Boink! Instant correction, and the dog did all the work.

Working with the leash dragging is also a good way to teach the dog to get into position when you command "heel." I require that my dogs stand beneath my left hand when I'm stopped and command "heel." When walking they can move a bit in front of me, but still on the left. So, no matter what I'm doing or what the dog is doing, when I call, then command the dog to "heel," I want the animal on my left. To teach that is a simple matter of encouraging the dog to move into that position by turning away from the animal and patting your hand against your left leg when you say "heel."

Here's how it's done. Command the dog to sit and back away. Call the dog. When the animal gets more than halfway to you, command "heel," turn your back to the dog and pat your left leg, so the dog comes to that spot. Then, just as the dog gets there, turn around again and pat your left leg, so the dog follows the patting sound behind you. When you stop moving, the dog should sit at your side. Then lavish on the praise. Incorporate several of these movements into each training session and pretty soon your dog will automatically fall in at your side when you say "heel."

That's really about all there is to teaching a dog to "heel." All of these practices can be applied not just during training sessions, but also during every walk in the park or trip around the block. Consistency is the key to success. If you refuse to let the dog yank at the leash and provide consistent commands and corrections, the fun will come back into those daily walks.

Chapter 8

Housebreaking (This is Important)

First things first: If your dog is going to live in your house or apartment, you have a vested interest in making sure the animal is adequately housebroken. That is, you will really want to train your dog to defecate and urinate outdoors. Training your dog to go on newspaper is not a substitute for housebreaking and can actually cause problems with your training program. If you have a really young puppy, you can use paper as an emergency measure, but your goal is to teach the dog to control her bodily functions until it is outside.

Most people buy puppies when they are about 8 weeks old. This is a very important time for the dog psychologically. Not only is the puppy in the middle of learning human socialization skills, but also the animal is very delicate when it comes to responding to fear. Harsh discipline at such an early age should be avoided, or it may impact the dog for months or years to come. So, you can start housebreaking the day you bring your puppy home but go easy on the discipline.

Dogs can be housebroken because they are, at their most basic level, den-dwelling animals. As such, dogs love to sleep in a warm, cozy den. Everything else happens outside the den. Dogs eat, socialize, mate and relieve themselves away from their dens. Dogs also love schedules. They fall very nicely into a routine. It provides structure, security and seems to give them a sense of understanding their environment. Putting a dog on a schedule for anything for a long enough time can make the actions of the

Your goal: To avoid any unpleasant surprises when you leave your dog in the house for an extended period. **What you'll need:** Patience, a good schedule and a dog box.

Dogs love to sleep in a warm and cozy den. This fact makes it very easy to housebreak a dog.

animal almost automatic. So that's where to start the housebreaking

The single most important aspect of house training is the schedule. Dogs typically have a bowel movement about 20 to 30 minutes after eating. With puppies, the interval can be even shorter, sometimes just a few minutes. This means you should plan your day and your training around regular feedings. And I do mean regular. If you are not maintaining the schedule of a German subway conductor, your housebreaking will suffer, and you'll have the carpet-cleaning bills to prove it. So, lay in an ample supply of good-quality dog food, feed amounts according to the label instructions or your veterinarian's recommendations, and establish a schedule that you are willing and able to maintain for several months. Don't panic, since the housebreaking should only take a week or two. But, maintaining the schedule will insure that you don't have to deal with any accidents from your young dog.

The Schedule

From 8 weeks to 3 months of age, you'll be feeding your puppy four times a day with meals in the morning, at noon, late afternoon and an hour before bedtime. The hour before bed allows the dog to digest

Only offer food and water for 20 minutes. That teaches the dog to eat and eventually go to the bathroom on your schedule.

the food and relieve himself prior to sleeping. Once the puppy passes 3 months, you can shift to a morning, after work and before bed feeding schedule. One of the keys to success will be to always take the young dog out soon after eating and drinking and encourage the dog to "do her business" outside.

Food and Water

Serve recommended portions of food, along with a bowl of water at the appointed times and make both available for only 20 to 25 minutes. Take away the bowls after 25 minutes, even if the dog hasn't finished eating all of the food. This will encourage the puppy to eat right away and allow you to stay on your schedule. There should be no free access to food at this time. I don't believe free-feeding is a great idea anyway, but it is especially bad when you are trying to housebreak a dog. And, don't go changing dog food brands in the middle of the housebreaking. A new kind of dog food can trigger diarrhea. Not only does that make it even harder for a young dog to "hold it," but the cleanup is not much fun either.

The Crate

Some call it a "den" or a dog box or a portable kennel. I call it a crate. Used in conjunction with the schedule, the crate will allow you to quickly housebreak the dog with very few accidents. Do not be cheap about dog crates. Get a good crate and get one that is right for your dog's current size. Don't buy one that's too big and wait for your dog to grow into it. Buy the right size and as the puppy grows, buy bigger crates. Although you might end up with three by the time the dog is fully grown, the headaches you'll save will be worth the cost.

The idea of the crate is that a dog will not soil his den. That's why dogs are so easy to housebreak. You can confine the dog in his crate while you are controlling the supply of food and water to teach the dog that relieving himself is something done only outside. The double bonus of using a crate is that during the training, the dog also learns to get over any separation anxiety early on. The best thing you can do for a young dog is allow the animal to be alone sometimes. Then, when you are gone to work, you won't have to deal with a lot of barking, chewing or other bad behavior. But that's for another chapter.

The Plan

So you've got the food and water, the crate and a general idea that you should follow a schedule. It will be tough for the first month, but by the time the puppy is 3 months old, she should have the muscle control to hold it for fairly long periods of time. That first month, expect some "accidents" and don't worry about discipline. The idea is to teach acceptable behavior, not change "bad" habits. For that first month, come home over lunch, hire a neighbor to take the puppy out and generally keep cleaning up while you work on the basics of feeding the puppy and taking him out a few minutes after he eats and drinks. At 3 months of age, you can start the real training. It will go something like this if you work during the day.

6:30 a.m.	Wake up and take puppy out immediately
6:45 to 7 a.m.	Playtime for puppy (with some supervision)
7 a.m.	Food and water
7:25 a.m.	Go out
7:45 a.m.	Into the crate
5:30 or 6 p.m.	Return from work and take puppy out immediately
6:15 p.m.	Playtime
6:30 p.m.	Into the crate
7:35 p.m.	Food and water
8 p.m.	Go out
8:15 to 8:30 p.m.	Playtime
8:30 p.m.	Into the crate
10:30 p.m.	Food and water
10:55 p.m.	Go out (be patient now and make sure the dog relieves himself)
11:30 p.m.	Into the crate for the night

Taking the dog to the same place each time you go out will make the housebreaking easier. Just remember, don't go too far or you'll have to go that far in the rain and snow, too.

During these playtime breaks, you should be working on the basic commands, especially "sit" as directed in Chapter 4. This is a great time to start some short training sessions. But keep them very short and play with the dog some, too.

While you are housebreaking the dog, you should only take her out to urinate and defecate. There should be no playtime outside. You are trying to convince the dog that outside is the place for her to relieve herself. It's also best to take the dog to the same general area each time you go out. That way the scent from previous outings will encourage the dog to go. Also, if the dog doesn't relieve himself within about 10 minutes after you go outside, take him back in and put him in the crate for about 10 minutes (but keep an eye on him). After a short time in the crate, take the dog out again. Also, remember to praise the dog intensely when she does her business in the right spot.

It should only take 10 to 12 days to housebreak a 3-month-old puppy with this method. Just remember to maintain the schedule, praise the positive work and clean the "accidents" thoroughly.

Adult Dogs

If you are trying to train an adult dog, perhaps one you rescued from the pound, the same principles apply. You do have a bit more leeway with timing and the duration of time between trips outdoors, but food control and confinement are the keys to success. Use the schedule above as a guideline and amend it to fit your daily routine but don't abandon it. Even if you only feed your adult dog one meal a day, the key to housebreaking will be regular use of the crate to encourage the dog to "hold it" and regular trips outdoors to show the dog the correct place to go. It may take a little longer to successfully break a fully-grown and untrained dog, but it can be done.

Urban Dwellers

Dogs living in the city have it a bit tougher than their country cousins. Plan your feeding and outside schedule to include "travel time" down the hall, into the elevator and out the door. Also, plan to carry your puppy all the way outside, especially first thing in the morning and after returning from work during the early stages of the training. This will prevent accidents on the way to the curb. Once outside, make sure your dog is on a leash at all times. You can use the leash to guide the dog to the curb and encourage her to relieve herself there, instead of in the middle of the sidewalk.

Another tip for city residents: Make the dog go close to the door to your apartment building. This will insure that you don't have to walk around the block if it is raining or snowing.

Crate time is very important for city dogs. Keeping the dog in the crate and showing no attention to whining or whimpering, will teach your dog that it's OK to be in the crate alone. And, you won't have to hear your neighbors complain that your lovable little puppy barked or howled all day.

Finally, make sure you clean up after your dog.

What if It Just Doesn't Work?

Effective housebreaking is based on the idea that you have a healthy dog. Most puppies should be able to hold it through the night by the time they are 15 weeks old if you let them go out just before bed and restrict water during the night. Some common dog maladies will throw your housebreaking program into disarray. Watch out for things like bladder infections that make it tough for a dog to hold urine for any length of time. Problems with digestion can show up as loose, runny stool. These are typically caused by changes in the diet, or because your dog was fed table scraps. Pay attention, however distasteful you find it, to the consistency of your dog's stools. If you haven't changed the dog's food and know there are no table scraps in the animal's diet, call your vet if your dog suffers from frequent loose stools.

There are plenty of other symptoms to pay attention to as well. If your dog is constipated or appears to be straining during defecation, you might need to contact your vet. Changes in eating or drinking habits or bad breath can also be a signal that something is not right. An acquaintance of mine once decided to take his dog to the vet to do something about the serious case of bad breath the dog was suffering from, and the doctor found a 3-inch stick lodged in the roof of the dog's mouth between his teeth. Vomiting, blood in the urine or stool or a temperature of more than 102 degrees are all reasons to have your dog checked by a vet right away.

Jealousy

Believe it or not, jealousy can play a role in housebreaking. More precisely, it can be the cause of accidents or slip-ups in an otherwise well trained dog. If your housebroken dog suddenly starts having accidents in the house, check to see if the accidents coincide with the arrival of anything that is directly competing with the dog for your attention. Another dog or a new puppy would be obvious, but realize too that a new baby can cause a dog to start wondering where he fits into the scheme of things, too.

To remedy slip-ups or accidents, maintain your schedule religiously and pay attention where you give your attention. If you are falling all over yourself to care for a new baby and forget about the dog, it's only natural for the dog to be confused about where he fits into the "pack," considering the devotion now being shown to the new arrival. Remember to include the dog in your activities with the baby and continue to encourage good behavior through praise.

If it's a new dog causing the problems, again, get back to a strict schedule. The easiest way is to include both dogs during the training of the newcomer. This will not only get the dogs used to being around one another, but it will also allow the veteran to "show" the new arrival how things work. The new dog will instinctively watch the actions of the other dog and follow suit as it works to find its place in the pack. This is also a time for careful supervision, especially during joint playtime because there are bound to be some dominance issues raised, especially if the dogs are close to the same size.

New House, New Training

You may also run into trouble with your dog if you move to a new house or apartment. Be prepared to get back to some serious scheduling and crate training, especially if you are moving from a quiet area to a noisy one. Moving to a new house means you are upsetting the familiarity your dog has with his current schedule. It can take a while to get things back on track. Be prepared for a few setbacks and plan accordingly. As always, consistency and diligence will be the keys to working through any problems.

Chapter 9

Dogs that Jump ... Must be Stopped

There is no delicate way to put it. Dogs that jump up on people are a pain. They are also annoying to everyone and can be dangerous, especially to the elderly and the very young. Swift retaliation is mandatory. Breaking a dog of this habit is not something I believe is open for discussion. A dog must not jump up on a human, ever. Period. No exceptions.

To get a handle on the jumping problem, let's first discuss what it is. A dog that jumps into the air when it is near a human is just an overly excited animal. A dog that jumps up and places her paws on a person (or a vehicle) is trying to establish dominance. Both of these situations are problems and must be corrected. The first situation is, quite simply, a dog out of control. The whole point of dog training is to control the dog. I like an energetic dog as much as the next person. But, a dog that is so excited that it's bouncing like a superball, will never listen to a command. You, as the handler, need to introduce and force the appropriate behavior.

The latter situation, in which the dog actually leaps up and puts his paws on a person, cannot be tolerated. This is a dog showing defiance of the established (well, it should be established) human/dog relationship in which the dog is always subordinate to the human, any human.

The long-standing rule has always been to "catch the dog in the act" of jumping and administer the corrections instantly. The correction is a raised knee that catches the

Your goal:
To avoid the dirty paws, scratching and annoying of visitors by an overly happy dog.
What you'll need:
Patience and good timing.

Dogs and kids are a perfect match, but only if the dog has learned that jumping is not allowed. For safety's sake, there can be no exceptions to this rule.

dog in the rib cage, right between and a bit behind the forelegs.

The raised knee must be supplied with sufficient force to not only get the dog's attention, but to also "discourage" future similar behavior. I'll be blunt; I've knocked some dogs completely over backwards with a well-timed knee. A couple of owners were a bit surprised to see Rover go flying, but they were equally surprised to see that Rover wasn't willing to jump on me the next time we met. There's a reason for that.

The reason the knee trick works so well is because the dog never sees it coming. No command is issued. There is no training session. There is nothing you really have to teach. All the dog knows is, "I jumped at that person, and when I did something hit me in the chest and knocked me down." It's as if the dog ran into a fence. You don't see that too often, do you? A dog might be running with his head down sniffing some great scent on the ground when "wham," he bonks right into a chain-link fence. That only happens once. The dog doesn't know what hit him; just that he got bonked when he was close to the fence. So he decided to be more careful near that fence. The same principle works with the knee trick.

There are some cautions to using the knee trick. The first one is that such a trick is not for the timid. You can't expect it to work if you are backing away from an out-of-control dog. You've got to step into the dog as the animal is coming up. You can't be cowering in fear. The second caution involves the amount of force you use. Don't overdo it. Just strike the dog hard enough to tip her back and get her off balance. The thump will sufficiently startle most dogs; it's not your job to inflict pain. The third caution involves how you follow up this action. Don't do anything. In no way should you indicate to the dog that you are responsible for the correction. You want the dog to believe the very act of jumping brought about the thump on the chest. That way the dog will quickly learn that jumping gets nothing but a startling pain in the chest.

If your dog jumps, greet him with a quickly raised knee. It won't be long before the dog stops jumping on you.

If someone else's dog jumps on you, try to catch the offending canine with a slap on the snout. Timing is important, but it really gets the dog's attention.

Other Situations

What about those other situations? What are they and how can you correct the behavior? As you can see, it's pretty easy to stop a dog from jumping up on you, especially if you're not bashful about lifting your knee with a bit of authority. But, what if your dog jumps on other people? I know it's difficult to even think about it, but admitting you have a problem is the first step to solving it.

If the dog is on a leash, things are going really well for you. I've said it before and I'll say it again. That leash gives you total control, so use it. If you know that your dog is a jumper, be prepared when you approach someone. At the first sign that your dog is preparing to jump, gather up the slack in the leash. You can usually tell the dog is about to lose control by the frantic tail wagging and general unruliness. So, shorten up on the leash. As the dog's paws come up, bend your knee (as if you are going to genuflect) and yank down on the leash as you issue a forceful verbal command "no."

In previous chapters, I've told you about corrections and using just enough force when you tug on the leash. In my world, all that goes out the window for a dog that jumps up. As far as I'm concerned, jumping up requires more than a correction; it requires a certified, attitude-adjusting punishment.

To double the impact, as you shout "no" rise to your feet and tower over the dog, looking as mean as you can look. The dog should know with every inch of his being that what he was trying to do was wrong. Immediately command the dog to sit and allow no movement. All the while you should try to look stern and menacing.

If the Dog is Off the Leash …

A jumper that is off the leash needs to be stopped just as effectively as one that is restrained. The problem is without a leash you have very little control. Here, I will contradict my previous statements and urge you to hit the dog. You'll be using an open-hand slap straight down on top of the dog's snout. There will be no punching, kicking, and hitting with any kind of hard object. Simply slap down on the dog's nose as it tries to jump. You will also be issuing the stern "no" command at this time, but there is a twist. When a dog is off the leash and you strike the animal's nose, you can expect it to cower and flee. As soon as this happens, command the dog to sit. Then be quiet and calm down for a minute. Do not, I repeat, do not attempt to call the dog to you for further punishment. It's foolhardy, bad for training and does not teach the dog anything useful. Once the dog is sitting and you've both calmed down, call the dog to your side and praise her as you normally would. What you want the dog to understand is that it was the jumping that drew the slap; everything else is fine. No jumping; no slap.

I suggest only using the slap technique on your own dog because you never know how someone is going to react to you striking his or her dog, even if the animal is about to jump on your child or companion. You'll never slap if the dog's jumping on you. In that case you'll raise your knee. You'll also never have to slap if your own dog is on a leash. So you can see this operation has very limited applications.

But it is effective because it provides instant negative response to the action you are trying to discourage.

As with any training, consistency is the key to keeping dogs from jumping up. I love dogs, but jumping is an action I will not tolerate from any dog. To stop it, you need to be firm and absolutely consistent. This can be a problem with kids around. I taught my 4-year-old son to never hit or hurt any dog, and then he saw me slap a yellow lab that was about to drive him into the ground. He didn't understand, and your kids may not either. The opposite might hold true if you have teenagers encouraging a dog to jump up for a hug or some rough play. In such a case, you've first got to teach the kids. I wouldn't recommend the knee in the chest or the slap technique on human students. Not even as a last resort.

Chapter 10

Every Dog's Favorite Game

These are the best fetch toys for dogs. Don't use a stick. It's an accident waiting to happen.

If your dog comes when you call, stands at your side when you command "heel" and sits on command, it's time to start working on the fancy stuff: Retrieving.

All dogs have the ability to retrieve. In fact, law enforcement agencies don't usually check pedigrees when they are looking for potential drug-sniffing dogs; they want a dog that will willingly and excitedly retrieve all day long. With that attitude, they can sculpt a canine cop.

You can teach any dog to fetch without much trouble at all, if you just continue building on the foundations we've already established. Remember, all we are trying to do is show the dog what we want, and then repeat the activity until it becomes second nature for the dog.

Your goal:
To throw an object and have your dog bring it right back to you.

What you'll need:
A dog, something to throw, a whistle and some treats.

Get the dog excited about chasing the dummy. This form of exercise and training should be fun for both dog and trainer.

Initial training to fetch, as with any type of training, should be done using the check cord.

My first rule of retrieving is this: It's only a game. So, I'll say it again: No hitting, shouting or pinching. It's all about making the dog want to bring something back to you.

The first part of retrieving is making sure the dog loves the game. The game has to be the greatest thing since doggie treats. Retrieving always has to be fun.

But, I'm getting ahead of myself. Let's start with something really simple. What should your dog fetch? First off, not sticks. A dog running with a stick in her mouth is an accident waiting for a big vet bill. You would never send your child to get you a long, pointed object and tell the kid, "Go get that! Run!" Not that I believe dogs and children are on the same level, but I do believe you should never do something you know has the potential to cause serious injury. So, you can use tennis balls, flying discs, a rolled-up towel secured with duct tape, a ball of twine ... just about anything that isn't sharp. My personal favorite is the product that is designed for just such an activity: the dog-training dummy or bumper. They are available at just about any sporting goods store or through most sporting goods mail-order or Internet retailers. Dummies come in a variety of sizes and colors and will nearly always stand up to the toughest dogs.

So, grab a retrievable item and get the dog excited about it. Start playing with the dog, swinging the dummy around the dog's nose and dragging it on the ground, just out of reach. Talk in an excited manner and try to keep the dog interested. If the dog is lucky enough to get hold of the dummy, don't pull it away. Just say, "Good dog!" and heap on the praise. Then, gently but firmly remove the dummy from her mouth and start again. While this is going on, drop in a "sit" command, just to reinforce old habits. You are doing this to remind the dog that even though something fun is happening, obedience must still be observed.

If the dog responds properly—and it should by this time—you are ready for your first toss. It will be a short one.

Put the dog on a long leash at "heel" and keep the animal by your side with a "sit" command. Toss the dummy 10 to 15 feet in front of the dog and hold the leash. Do not let the dog rush off until you say. After a short wait (five or 10 seconds), give the command "fetch" and

Send the dog for a short retrieve. If she doesn't come right back, pull on the cord.

point to the dummy. As soon as the dog picks up the dummy, call her back. If everything goes according to plan, the dog should come right back. If not, you can pull on the rope to reel her in.

Now, you have to get the dummy. This is the only place I will get a bit forceful with a dog. For me, a game of tug of war is not part of learning to retrieve. But it may be for you. If you want the dog to deliver fetched objects right to your hand and let go on command, tell the dog "give" and immediately take the dummy. If the dog does not want to let go, grab the lower jaw and squeeze a bit while you pull down. As soon as the dummy is in your hand, praise the dog lavishly.

Teaching Good Habits

During this cycle of training, it is especially important to create good habits and be careful not to instill any bad ones.

Good habits include:

- Waiting until the fetch command is given to break for the dummy.
- Running right to the dummy, picking it up and running right back to you.
- Holding the dummy until you take it.
- Giving up the dummy on command.

Anything else is a bad habit. Do not allow it. So, here are some tips for creating these good habits.

Steadiness

Give the "sit" command before each toss. If the dog breaks after the throw, but before the "fetch" command, call her back (or pull on the long check cord) and give the command again. Wait five seconds. Point to the dummy and say "fetch."

Two things are really important here. Don't be too firm in commanding the dog, especially a young dog, if he breaks with the throw. Remember, this is to be fun. But also don't let the dog

PHOTO BY SARA VAN ASTEN

Part of the game is for the dog to give you the dummy. Don't play tug of war, here. On the command "give" the dog should release the dummy.

Once you've taught your dog to stay, you can throw the dummy and wait a bit before sending him to get it.

get away with running to the dummy until you command it. Then, don't wait too long before giving the "fetch" command. Young dogs might forget you tossed the dummy. As the dog gets older, you can wait longer and longer to send the animal. For now, keep the wait just long enough to let the dog know you are in command.

Another way to steady the dog is to command "sit," toss the dummy and go get it yourself. Don't let the dog get up, reinforce the command if you need to and pick up the dummy and toss it again. Then say "fetch."

Straight-There and Straight-Back

On these early tosses, straight-there should be no problem. If it is a problem, shorten up the toss even more, point to the dummy and say "fetch." Straight-back should just be your dog's response to the "come" command. If the dog runs off, go get him and run the drill on a long lead so you can reel him in.

Holding the Dummy

If the dog picks up the dummy and drops it, you've got some work to do. Get the dog at "heel," standing next to you. Hold the dummy in your hand and say "fetch." Then put the dummy into the dog's mouth. If he drops it, say, "No, fetch," and put the dummy back in the dog's mouth. Then, wait five seconds and say "give" and take the dummy. Slowly work up to longer and longer times that you require the dog to hold the dummy. After several training sessions, your dog should hold that dummy as long as you can stand to wait. Then, he'll release it precisely on command. When the dog has that mastered, toss the dummy, say "fetch" and see what happens.

Retrieving a dummy can be hard work. Give your dog a chance to rest when she needs it.

A flying disc is a safe and fun alternative to dummies. It gives the dog something else to chase and another reason to have fun.

When the dog runs straight to get the dummy and comes straight back, the game is much more fun for the trainer. Teach this early by training with the check cord, and then enforce it every time you play.

During all of this training session, I've quietly stressed pointing at the dummy as you give the command to "fetch." The dog will see you pointing now and always find something fun (in this case, the dummy) in the direction you are pointing. It won't take long for a young dog to figure out that by heading in the direction you point, he will find something he likes. And when he brings it back and gets that pat on the head, he'll feel like he just won the lottery. A dog that works that happily should be your ultimate goal.

Build on Your Foundation

All of these training sessions give you the perfect opportunity to build on the other blocks in the training foundation. During these early retrieval sessions, don't hesitate to spring some of the other commands on the dog or stop tossing the dummy to work on the previous commands you feel you have mastered. Keep your whistle with you for every training session and be consistent. By really training the dog for 15 minutes and playing with the animal for another five to 15 minutes, you will be building bonds that will stay with the dog to his dying day.

Other Fun Fetch Games

If you don't have a dummy and don't want to get one, a tennis ball makes a pretty good substitute. And there are some games you can play with a tennis ball that just don't work with a retrieval dummy. The bouncing ball is one of them. Try bouncing a dummy and you won't have much fun at all. But, with a tennis ball, you can get your dog all stirred up and excited, then whip the ball hard right at the ground and say "sit" as the ball bounces skyward. As it comes down for the first bounce, give the "fetch" command. With some dogs, catching the bouncing ball can really be a great test of agility. And it's really fun to watch.

Throwing a flying disc for a dog was popularized a couple decades ago when a few nimble dogs were seen making acrobatic catches during the halftime shows at football games. It's true that you can

Dogs love to chase flying discs. It is safe, healthy and fun.

to accomplish such feats, but the reality is that it takes an impressive combination of training, athleticism and skill to pull this off. In short, you need the right kind of dog, good training and you need to learn to throw the disk just about perfectly. I personally have never owned a dog with that kind of leaping ability (unless he was trying to scale a kennel fence). And I've never been able to throw a Frisbee that well.

Now that's not to say I haven't had fun throwing one for the dog. It just seems that I've never been able make the connection that gets me on the highlight films. Most of the time, my dogs run alongside the flying disk until it lands and scratch at it on the ground until they can pick it up and bring it back. The whole process is carried out much the same way I would train the dog to retrieve a dummy, except that I give the fetch command while the Frisbee is still flying.

Water Retrieves

The first time you try to get your dog into the water, you might want to make sure that you either have your swimming suit on or that the thing you're about to throw is something you don't mind losing.

Some dogs take to water like fish. Others need to be convinced that water is fun. It's not a difficult task—most of the time. There are some instances, though, that can be challenging.

The one thing you don't want to do is rush a dog that shows any hesitation about going into the water. If you pick up your dog and drop him off a dock, you could end up with an animal that suffers from a severe phobia. So take it slowly. Start at the water's edge with your dog's favorite fetch toy and you in your swimming suit.

The first thing to do is take the dog's mind off the water. Do this by teasing the dog with the dummy, getting the animal all excited, and then tossing the dummy right on the edge of the water. The goal is to place the dummy in the water, but so close the dog can reach it without getting too wet. As soon as the dog grabs the dummy, lavish the animal with praise. Then, do it again and again, making tosses into deeper water so the dog has to wade out a bit to get the dummy. Once the dog is confident charging into water up to her belly, it's time for you to get wet.

Wade out into knee-deep water while teasing the dog with the dummy. Make your first toss parallel to shore and excitedly encourage the dog to go for the dummy. As the dog goes into the water, you walk to shore to receive the dummy. Keep tossing deeper and deeper, until the dog is swimming for the dummy. At this point, you're about done. All you have to do is keep making longer and longer throws into the deep water. The dog will figure out what to do.

Don't Overdo It

Fetch is a game that most dogs will love, but you can get too much of a good thing. As I said at the beginning, law enforcement agencies look for dogs that willingly will fetch until your arm is tired. This means not all dogs will do this. Too much of the game, especially on hot days or with long water retrieves, can tire a dog to the point that she will not go on.

Don't run your dog to the point of exhaustion because once he lies down and realizes that he doesn't really have to fetch things for you, it might be the end of the game—permanently. Keep the sessions to about 10 or 15 minutes, and then break up the activity with some other sort of play. You can go back to fetching things later, but don't overdo it during one session. Remember, it's a game. It's supposed to be fun.

Chapter 11

Quiet: It Can Be Taught

What are dogs thinking? Sometimes you can tell by the way they bark. Most of the other times they have that same look on their faces.

Dogs bark. To quote one of my father's favorite sayings, "There ain't no two ways about it." Dogs bark. Sometimes that's good. A barking dog is a prowler's biggest problem. Thousands of people buy dogs each year because dogs provide some level of protection just by making noise when something is out of the ordinary. People lurking in the dark like it quiet and dogs, especially smaller breeds, can shatter that quiet in a hurry with a sound most people notice.

As in most cases, too much of a good thing can cause some rather serious problems, especially for suburbanites and urban apartment dwellers. When a dog starts barking in a subdivision or an apartment, people tend to want that dog to be silenced right away. These situations can get downright tense. Police regularly respond to "barking

Your goal:
To keep your dog from barking every time you leave.
***What* you'll need:**
A dog, a dog box and patience.

dog" complaints and friendships have been torn apart because one neighbor has a barking dog and the other works nights and is trying to get some sleep. On the other side of the coin, those who live in rural areas often don't have to deal with the problem of a barking dog with any great urgency. Would you believe, that is precisely what helps the dog learn to stop barking?

Good Barking or Bad?

If you've been around dogs for some time, you know what barking is. If you've paid any attention at all to the specific sounds a particular dog makes while barking, then you know barking is the canine equivalent of a mass communications course. You've got your, "feed me" bark and the "I'm lonely" bark and the "let's play" bark. There are likely dozens of others, but the one bark we all seem to understand is the one that means something is wrong. I'm all in favor of doing away with all other forms of barking. If my dogs are warning me of impending danger, fine. I'll put up with their barking. Barking for any other reason is not allowed.

Dogs can get lonely. Early training helps them to understand that being alone is not something to bark about.

Sometimes grasping the snout and giving a firm command will get a dog to understand that barking is not the right thing to do.

Most of the time, that incessant daytime barking - the kind that drives everyone nuts – is caused by separation anxiety. That is, your dog is upset because you are not around. You might just say, "Oh well, I'm not around, let him bark." Well, aside from being downright abusive to your neighbors, a dog that barks nonstop is just one step away from chewing, clawing and generally terrorizing your house or his kennel. I always believed a dog would not cause himself pain. That is, until I had a German shorthair pointer that was desperate to be by my side. The dog completely destroyed a chain-link kennel and any means of reinforcement I could come up with. Day after day, I would come home to find the dog waiting on the back steps of my house, bloodied from his battle with the chain-link kennel. It all started with excessive barking and my failure to correct it while the dog was young.

To eliminate separation anxiety, you've got to start early and impress upon the dog that being alone is not such a bad thing. Teaching this is important because, as you remember from earlier in the text, the dog is a pack animal. Without the pack, the dog feels alone. You represent the pack, and the dog wants to be with you to understand his place in the pack. So, you need to incrementally introduce the dog to the idea that being isolated is nothing to bark about. This is where the crate training for housebreaking comes in so handy. Between the times when the dog is eating, taking short play breaks and actually going outside to urinate or defecate, the dog should be in the box. Go about your business in the house, but ignore the dog. The noise you make will reassure the dog that you are nearby. That should be enough of a calming influence, especially when the dog is young.

This time in the crate allows the dog to come to view the crate as her den. The crate is a safe and quiet place for the dog to simply relax and wait for you. Don't spoil that. If the dog whines or barks from inside the crate when you are near, ignore it. Let the dog learn that barking brings nothing. One of the worst things you can do to a dog that whines or barks in the crate is walk over, bang on the crate and holler, "shaddup!" Do this and it won't be long before your dog understands that barking will get your attention. That will cause the dog to bark more. Then, you are taking away the animal's safe haven by banging on the box and yelling at the dog. Such action could put the dog off the whole idea of going into the crate at all. When the dog is in the crate, stick to the regular training schedule for housebreaking, and you should at the same time be teaching the dog that being alone is nothing to worry about.

Lots of romping around can create a hyper dog. Sometimes you just have to ignore the animal a bit to reinforce the idea that calm is better.

What if That Doesn't Work?

Well, if you've got a puppy that still insists on barking, or an older dog that seems to be a slow learner, you might have to get a bit more physical. No hitting is involved, but you will have to grab the dog firmly but gently by the snout and, while holding the upper and lower jaws together, issue a firm "no." Make sure you don't have any lip tissue caught between the dog's teeth when you grab the upper and lower jaws, as pinching the dog's tender lips will cause some real problems between you and your dog.

Only try this method if ignoring the dog has not worked. That's because the downside of grasping the snout means you are giving the dog some sort of attention and that, after all, is exactly what the animal wants. So, to do it correctly, you need to be firm and brief. Say, "no!" just once, perhaps including a good menacing stare, then go back to ignoring him. Whatever you do, don't let the dog out of the crate while you are providing this type of correction. Just open the gate a bit, and as the dog tries to come out, grab the snout, issue the command and send the dog back into the kennel. Then walk away. This kind of training takes patience and the ability to sit by and do nothing while the dog barks. It can be frustrating, but just keep it up. The dog will get the idea eventually.

Teaching a dog to speak on command is also a good way to keep a dog from barking. If the dog barks to get a treat, and there is no treat, then there is no reason to bark.

It pays to know a little about the breed you might want. This big German shorthair pointer likes to run and will need more than average exercise. Do some research before you decide on a breed.

Coming Home to a Hyper Dog

You can unwittingly help create a case of separation anxiety by being overjoyed to see your dog when you come home from work each day. The scenario might go something like this: After a hard day at work, you head straight home to let the dog out and allow the beauty of some canine companionship wash away the worries of a tough day. So, you come home, immediately let the dog out and then commence to playing your dog's favorite game. There is a lot of romping, happy talk and general frivolity. Let's say you have a really bad couple of weeks, and you do this every night for two weeks. One day, you come home and notice that your dog is so excited that the animal is literally bouncing off the walls of the crate waiting for you to play. Well, that night you can't play. The dog gets a quick trip outside, and then it's back in the kennel while you prepare for a dinner meeting or something. Your dog might decide it's time to start barking.

That's because you've established a routine, and now you are deviating from it, making the dog a bit uptight. To nip this in the bud, you've got to remember to include some random periods of silence for the dog after you come home from work. To be good about it, come home, let the dog out to urinate and/or defecate, and then it's right back into the crate while you change clothes. This lets the dog know that you are setting the schedule and you'll arrange for playtime. It shows the dog that if you don't let her out to play as soon as you get home, things will still be just fine.

It's Always Something ...

The flip side of this type of training can also be used on dogs that are already habitually hyper. Keep the dog in the crate when you get home from work. If the dog gets hyper inside the crate, issue the command "sit" just once. Wait for the dog to sit, and as soon as the animal does, open the crate. As you work toward calming the dog, you add increasing amounts of time that the dog must remain quiet before you let him out. Doing so reinforces the fact that the correct behavior (being quiet) is the only one that gets any response. And that gets the best response of all, a chance to get out and rejoin the pack.

An Alternate Method

If you feel like you want to try something totally different, you can quiet a dog by teaching him to bark. It sounds odd, but it does work with some dogs and some trainers. I've had mixed success with the system and believe that the times it's worked have included another training step that I didn't know I was applying at the time of the training. But anyway, here's the system in a nutshell.

You get some treats and teach the dog to bark on command. You simply hold up the treat and tease the dog until the animal makes a noise, then you give the treat. You can make up your own command, but most people will use "speak." Withhold the treat until the dog actually barks, then give the treat and lots of praise. In no time at all your dog will be barking on command. That's the trick. You've taught your dog to bark on command in order to get a treat. Keep this up, stressing the training on the dog and soon the dog will not bark without hearing the command. If the dog is trained to bark on command and the reward is a treat, then if there is no command, no one to give the command and no chance to get the treat, the dog sees no need to bark.

I know, it's an odd system that uses some really obvious reverse psychology. It can be effective and several trainers recommend such training, especially for dogs that tend to respond well to other commands but, for some reason, can't remain quiet when alone. Try it. It could work. And even if it doesn't, you've taught your dog a new trick. 🦴

Chapter 12

Traveling with Your Dog

Creating a safe and comfortable place in the vehicle is the best way to introduce your dog to traveling.

On the Road

With few exceptions, dogs can go anywhere their masters go. You just have to plan ahead and remember to think about how and where the dog fits into your travel plans.

So, let's look at the mode of transportation most of us will be using on a regular basis — the automobile.

A few years back, there was an advertising campaign for a major carmaker that included the tagline, "Dogs lo-o-ove trucks." Well, most of them love cars, too. Your average dog is more than happy to hop into the family

Your goal:
To make the trip enjoyable for you and your dog.
What you'll need:
A dog box, a leash, food, water, a dog toy and some planning.

Before you get going, give the dog time to "go." It will make traveling easier.

This is no way to travel, and it's not even safe to leave a dog like this in a parked vehicle. Use the dog box while traveling and never leave a dog in a parked car or truck.

sedan and go for a ride. But traveling any distance with a canine companion takes a bit more planning than does a trip with only human companions. And with some dogs, even short trips can be a hassle.

When I was a kid, we owned an Irish setter that would drool incessantly as soon as the car started moving. It was not a pretty sight, as everyone tried to get as far away from the dog as possible. I've also heard about (but never actually seen) dogs that get carsick and vomit once a vehicle starts moving. With possibilities like these, you have some experimenting to do before you start out on a long trip. That is, start with a few short trips to see how your dog reacts to riding in a motor vehicle.

The first order of business is to make a safe and comfortable place for your pet inside the vehicle.

Far and away the best option is a portable kennel. This, of course, depends on the size of your dog and the size of your vehicle. If you own a St. Bernard and a Geo Metro, you'll not likely be able to fit a portable kennel of adequate size into the cargo bay. Make sure everything fits. Then, arrange the kennel so the opening is near a door or the rear hatch. Insert your dog's bed, favorite blanket or the pad that came with the kennel and call the dog. If you have used the portable kennel for other training, your dog will surely hop right in. Securely latch the kennel door and you are nearly ready to get on your way. I say "nearly ready" because you should really take one last look at things, even if only to make sure the portable kennel is stable. Nothing can spoil a dog from riding in a car or truck like a wobbly kennel. Worse yet is having a kennel tip over.

Before putting the dog into the car or truck for a trip of any length, make sure the animal has a chance to defecate and urinate. Be patient and give the dog a few minutes. If you get no response, go ahead and load up for your trip.

There's really nothing special about driving with a canine co-pilot, but if the dog is in a kennel and the kennel is not supported, watch the speed on corners. I once tossed my poor German shorthair pointer from one side of the truck bed to the other, not even knowing I was taking the corners too quickly. Apparently the dog

A good kennel that's the right size for the dog is a must for any airline travel. Contact your travel agent in advance to find out all the rules.

stood up, which changed the center of gravity in the kennel. One corner got the ball rolling, so to speak.

The real key to driving with a dog is what you do when you stop, even if it is just to get some gas. The first thing on your mind the moment you stop should be to let the dog out to relieve herself. There's something about riding in a car or truck that makes a dog really have to go the moment the vehicle stops. So, when you pull in for gas, swing around behind the station first. Let the dog out (on a leash, of course) and allow the animal take care of business. After that is out of the way, load the dog and head for the fuel pumps.

If, while you are driving, you notice the dog panting a lot, make sure you give her some water to drink. Some dogs get agitated and pant excessively while riding in a vehicle. Excessive panting expels plenty of water vapor, and it won't take long for the dog to get dehydrated. In such an instance, it is a good idea to offer the dog water every few hours while on the road.

At the other end of the spectrum, some dogs simply relax and fall asleep while riding. I've gone as many as eight hours at a stretch with dogs that simply relax and enjoy the ride. In this type of situation, it pays to take a bit of a longer break when you do stop. At such time, offer the dog water and food. And, a short walk is always good for both pet and pet owner after several hours in the car.

For trips that conclude within 10 to 12 hours of driving, I typically restrict food until we get to the destination. The dog won't starve, and it makes things easier for me. On cross-country trips, you can establish your own feeding schedule, but remember

Before long trips, especially by air, feed your dog at least an hour before you depart.

to allow the dog enough time during the stop to relieve herself. This can take up to 30 minutes after eating for some dogs. Don't be in such a hurry that you force the dog back into the kennel and head on down the road with an accident waiting to happen in the dog box. Such incidents are messy, irritating for both you and the dog, and are very rarely ever the dog's fault.

Some dog owners let their pets ride around unsecured inside automobiles. Of such activity, I will say only this: It is an option, but it's not a very good one.

Blankets on the back seat; a dog sitting on the driver's lap and the oft-seen dog with its head out the window are common, but none are healthy or safe for the dog. Dogs are most comfortable and secure in the confines of a portable kennel. The dog will not get in your way as

As soon as you can after you arrive, get your dog out for some exercise and the chance to relieve himself.

Call in advance to see if your hotel allows dogs. If so, a dog bed is a good idea but bringing your portable kennel into the room might be better.

you steer and nothing will be flying into the animal's ears and eyes as you speed down the highway. I could preach, but I'm not going to. Just put the dog in a portable kennel that is the correct size for the animal's current weight.

There are also any number of great pet travel products on the market. From spill-proof water containers to self-contained feeding stations to disposable clean-up kits that allow for quick and efficient disposal of accidents. Shop wisely for these items and remember that everything you buy is one more thing to carry during your trip.

Taking to the Air

Airline travel with a dog can be a bit of a hassle, but it can be done. The first thing you need to do is alert your travel agent or ticket clerk very early in the process that you intend to travel with a dog. At that time, you will be given a printed copy of the policies of your specific airline and you'll also very likely be given some tips to make the trip better for both you and your dog. Follow these tips!

The first thing you'll need is a portable kennel that meets or exceeds airline specifications. Buy a good kennel that is the right size for your dog. If you have a really small dog, you might be able to bring the kennel with you as a carry-on bag. This might be comforting for the dog, but then again, it may cause problems with the other passengers if your dog decides she isn't enjoying the flight. A courteous dog owner considers others. So, think about it.

My suggestions for a portable kennel to be used for airline travel are limited to the plastic versions with metal wire doors. The wire kennels just don't give dogs enough privacy. The hustle and bustle of the air terminal, the rough handling by the baggage smashers, and the noise and vibration of takeoffs and landings all add stress to your dog's trip. When a dog is stressed, she just wants to curl up in a safe, secure place and hide. The nearly solid walls of the plastic kennels provide more privacy for your pet than do wire cages.

As for actually traveling by air with your dog, the biggest issue is time. Start early. Feed your dog a nutritious meal of his regular dog food at least an hour before you depart for the airport. Offer water and allow the dog to go outside to defecate and urinate before your trip begins. Most airports don't have adequate green space for walking dogs, so if your drive to the airport is a long one, make plans for a short stop at a park or other "dog-friendly" area to give your pet one last chance to relieve himself before you arrive at the airport. Restrict water and food from this time on.

If your trip includes long flights or extended layovers, make sure you tell your ticket agent you are traveling with a pet and will need to care for the animal. Most baggage is checked right through to your destination, but if time and facilities permit, you should make every effort to care for your dog during a long stop. It might be a hassle for ticket agents and baggage handlers, but you should insist.

Soft bedding and a favorite toy should be included in the portable kennel for the flight. Some animals will also feel more secure if you include an article of your clothing. It will help the dog, but you can consider that shirt suitable for nothing but the trash once you get to your destination. So choose the clothing wisely.

Once you arrive, get your dog some exercise and water as soon as you can. Most airports require that dogs remain kenneled while in the terminal, but you can—and should—snap on a leash as soon as you make it to the sidewalk. Praise the dog. Be friendly for a while, and then act as if the trip was really no big deal. In most cases, airline travel for a dog is nothing more than a bumpy, noisy stay in the kennel and usually doesn't last any longer than your typical day at work. Most dogs can handle it just fine.

Be aware that there may be additional vaccination and even quarantine requirements, especially when flying to foreign countries. Make sure to ask about such requirements and keep all the mandatory paperwork within easy reach. It is not a bad idea to safeguard your dog's papers just as diligently as you do your own passport and airline tickets.

Suitable Lodging

In the United States, public opinion seems to be that dogs and hotels don't mix. Don't you believe it! The American Automobile Association (AAA) has a book listing more than 10,000 pet-friendly AAA-rated hotels. AAA's book is now in its fourth edition, so in this case, I leave that research to the acknowledged travel masters. The book includes a list of dog parks in the U.S. and Canada. There are also listings for animal clinics across the country, tips for selecting an airline and choosing an appropriate travel crate, plus pet safety guidelines for traveling by car or plane. AAA members pay $12.75 and nonmembers pay $15.95.

Even if you get the book, it always pays to call ahead and ask about the hotel's pet policy. It might cost you a few dollars more, or you might have to pay an additional deposit, but at least everyone will know what's going on before you arrive. What you'll want to do is ask for a room on the first floor, preferably near an exit. That way, trips outside will be quick and easy.

It's a good idea to bring your portable kennel right into the hotel room with you. That way, your dog has a comfortable place to stay in her new surroundings. It also gives you a safe area for your dog if you wanted to leave the room without her. There is nothing worse than leaving your dog in a hotel room so you can get dinner, only to find that the anxiety of staying in a strange new place has prompted your dog to trash the room. You'll also want to make sure your dog knows it is supposed to remain quiet while you are gone. Can you imagine the look on the hotel manager's face if your dog has been howling the entire time you were gone? You'd surely be looking for another room.

Basic Dog Travel Checklist

- Be sure your dog follows all basic obedience commands.
- Ensure your dog is healthy enough to travel. (If you are concerned, call your vet.)
- Research any special animal regulations at your destination.
- Get a copy of your pet's shot records.
- Select a crate approved by the United States Department of Agriculture Animal and Plant Health Inspection Service (USDA-APHIS).
- Carry plenty of your dog's food.
- Get copies of airline transport regulations.
- Try not to leave your pet alone in the hotel. If you must, crate or otherwise confine her. Crate at night, too.
- Leave a "do not disturb" sign on your door. Keep your pet and the housekeeper from an unpleasant surprise.
- Notify management immediately if something is damaged. Be ready to pay for repairs.
- Add a little extra to the housekeeping tip.
- Bring a leash and use it.
- Get the dog an identification tag with your name and full address. ⊂⊃

Chapter 13

Canine Nutrition: A Brief Look

Food is Serious Business

Look at the information on page 121. There, we've taken all the fun out of feeding your dog. Now we can go about feeding correctly for a long life and good health.

The best way to get people interested in canine nutrition is to link that which your dog takes in to that that which you dog puts out. Are you with me? Good food really can reduce the amount of poop you have to clean up. Now you're paying attention. In addition to the input/output equation, proper nutrition is a key element in the health and long life of your dog. Luckily, there is a world of information out there ... so much so that I'll just touch on the highlights here.

Dogs require six types of nutrients: water, protein, fat, carbohydrates, minerals and vitamins. Those commercial pet foods billed as 100 percent complete and balanced provide all of a dog's requirements, except water. Even if you provide the best, most complete, most expensive dog food available, you will be shortchanging your dog's health without clean, fresh drinking water.

Water

Let's start with the one thing all animals need. Water is everywhere. Cells are pretty much made of water inside and out. Water is involved in some way in just about every chemical and biological reaction in the body. In short, water is required for good health. Water is the most important nutrient for survival on a short-term basis, and it is one that is too frequently neglected.

Water is the key to a dog's ability to regulate body temperature. Because water is needed for just about everything, any big change in water consumption can cause

Your goal: To maintain a healthy, balanced diet.
What you'll need: Good dog food, common sense and a veterinarian.

Some Facts About Feeding a Dog

- Table scraps will not provide the balanced diet dogs need. Ideally, table scraps should not be fed. If you do offer them, table scraps should never make up more than 10 percent of the dog's daily food intake.
- Feeding a dog raw eggs repeatedly can cause a deficiency of the vitamin biotin. Raw egg whites contain avidin, an enzyme that stops biotin from being absorbed into the body. Symptoms of biotin deficiency include dermatitis (inflammation of the skin), loss of hair and poor growth.
- Although dogs may enjoy meat, it is not a balanced diet. Raw meats may contain parasites, and cooked meats can be high in fat and do not contain a proper balance of nutrients.
- Some raw fish can cause a deficiency of the vitamin thiamine. Symptoms of a thiamine deficiency include anorexia (complete loss of appetite), abnormal posture, weakness, seizures and even death. Raw salmon will also transmit deadly parasites.
- Raw liver, fed daily in large quantities, can cause a vitamin A toxicity in dogs. This is particularly true if it is fed along with a complete and balanced diet already containing ample vitamin A.
- Milk is a food and not a substitute for water. As a food, milk is incomplete and does not provide a balanced diet. It can be useful as a treat for some dogs; however, large quantities of milk may not be well tolerated. Milk contains lactose, which requires the enzyme lactase digestion. If the intestinal tract does not contain sufficient lactase, a high level of lactose can cause diarrhea.
- Small soft bones (such as pork chops or chicken bones) should never be given to dogs, as they may splinter and lodge in the mouth or throat.

problems. So, animals have evolved great ways to help them keep things in balance. But remember, access to water is paramount.

- Dogs get water from the water they drink, fluid swallowed with food, and water generated from metabolic activity inside the body.
- Water is lost to urination, bowel movement, respiration, and to a much lesser extent, in saliva and nasal secretions. For nursing females, water will also be required for milk production.
- Work, even growing, gestating and lactation, and the temperature and humidity all have an impact on how much water a dog needs. Generally, the more a dog eats, the more water it needs. So, it stands to reason that larger dogs need more water than smaller breeds. But

This is training, too. If you require that your dog sit and wait to be fed, things get much easier at feeding time.

GUARANTEED ANALYSIS:

Crude Protein (Min)	21.0%	Linoleic Acid (Mir
Crude Fat (Min)	10.0%	Calcium (Ca) (Mir
Crude Fiber (Max)	4.5%	Phosphorus (P) (
Moisture (Max)	12.0%	Vitamin A (Min)

INGREDIENTS: Ground yellow corn, poultry by-pr animal fat preserved with mixed-tocopherols (forr soybean meal, dicalcium phosphate, animal dige: arley flour, salt, potassium chloride, L-Lysine hloride, zinc sulfate, Vitamin E supplement, zinc lethionine, added color (Red 40, Yellow 5, I anganese proteinate, niacin, Vitamin A supplemen lfate, calcium pantothenate, copper protein drochloride, Vitamin B-12 supplement, thiamin

Read the label. Good dog food will list all the ingredients. If you have questions, ask your vet.

with all of the other conditions previously mentioned, it's best to have a ready source of fresh, clean water available at all times. Don't be alarmed if your dog drinks a lot one day and a bit less or more the next. If there is more water in the food, the dog needs to drink less. That's why dogs eating canned dog food usually don't spend as much time at the water bowl. Canned food contains about 75 percent water, and dry food has about 8 percent to just over 10 percent. It's easy to see where things can be vary.

The variables also include the age of the dog. A growing puppy requires up to four times more energy per pound of body weight than a full-grown dog. As the puppy approaches adulthood, you can cut back on the calories. That's why you feed puppy food to puppies and to pregnant females. At the end of gestation and during lactation, that new mom also needs between two and four times more food/ nutrition than a normal, healthy adult dog.

Dogs that live outside and have to deal with changes in temperature also require changes in their diets. When it's hot, you can typically feed a dog a little less because they don't need as much energy to keep warm. But remember the water. Drinking plenty of fresh water is the best way for a dog to keep cool. As you would guess, more food is needed when it gets cold outside, but that doesn't mean you should skimp on water. Water helps the dog to digest and metabolize the food. So, water is just as important in keeping a dog warm as it is to keeping a dog cool.

Hard at Work

Hard work, like including the training sessions that lead up to hard work, put great demands on dogs, and they need more food and water because of it. The folks at Purina put together a set of standards for working dogs through scientific experiments with dogs on treadmills running the equivalent of 20 miles per day at 75 degrees. Again, and some would say rather obviously, dogs working hard need high-calorie, nutrient-dense foods and lots of them. While you can't replicate such experiments at home, when you plan to start working your dog hard, plan ahead and slowly make the switch to a high-protein dog food.

Protein is the Key

All good-quality dog foods will tell you how much protein they contain. Some brag about it, and others put it in small print. Protein is essential for things like muscle growth, blood, immune functions, energy and all kinds of good things. A dog's protein requirement depends on activity level and age of the dog. Puppies need more dietary protein than adult dogs. Food requirements are also high for puppies. A high-quality source of protein that makes up 20 to 25 percent of the calories taken in will usually meet the needs of a puppy.

It might come as a surprise, but old dogs also need more protein. They need about 50 percent more than do younger adult dogs. The key is to pay attention to your dog's weight and condition and get regular veterinary checkups.

Severe protein deficiency (starvation, really) in dogs results in poor food intake, retarded growth or weight loss, muscle wasting, emaciation and death. Before it gets that bad, you will see things like a rough, dull coat, problems with the immune system and poor milk

Switching Dog Foods

You can't switch dog foods overnight. Your dog will end up with gastric "distress." It's runny. It's messy. It's no fun for you or the dog. So here's the plan: switch foods slowly. Start out with a ratio of new food to old in the 1:4 range. That's one cup of new food mixed with four cups old. Then over the next week or two change the ratio to 1:2 and 1:1 and 2:1. Once you get to where you are serving two cups of new food mixed with one cup of old, you can pretty much make the jump all the way to the new stuff. Still, keep an eye on the output (as if you could not notice that kind of stuff) and make double sure the dog has plenty of water.

Choose a good-quality food and stock up. If you change brands, do it slowly so you do not to upset the dog's digestive system.

production in moms with puppies that are nursing. Dogs that seem to get along fine but are provided with less protein than they need may appear healthy, but are most susceptible to infections and are more likely to get cancer.

While more than 20 amino acids are involved in the synthesis of proteins in dogs, 10 of them are called "essential" because enough of

Essential amino acids include:

- arginine
- histidine
- isoleucine
- leucine
- lysine
- methionine
- phenylalanine
- threonine
- tryptophan
- valine

them cannot be formed fast enough to meet the dog's dietary needs and must be supplied constantly through a good-quality food.

Scientists at Purina have found, as one would guess, that when dogs work or play hard, they need more protein. Pregnant and nursing dogs also need more protein. For example, a dog food containing at least 21 percent protein (dry-type dog food) is recommended for reproduction. Hard-working dogs also need more calories and more fat. Check with your veterinarian as to what is right for your dog and

Treats can encourage even the most stubborn dog to listen to anyone. Just don't overdo it.

her unique situation. There really is no one-size-fits-all solution.

On the other side of the coin, dogs that don't get much exercise need the food that is lower in fat and calories and may have a lower protein level. The food should also contain a higher percentage of crude fiber. Perhaps it could go without saying, but I'll say it anyway: pay attention to what you are feeding; read the labels. A low-calorie pet food is not right for puppies or for pregnant or nursing females.

Sources

Proteins are derived from both animal and plant sources, and you'll get extremists on both sides of the issue. Some claim dogs, as descendants of wolves, should eat only meat. The vegan crowd would disagree and there are, indeed, vegetarian dog foods and treats. The truth is, most proteins don't contain adequate amounts of one or

Puppies should eat puppy food. They have different nutritional requirements than adult dogs, and only puppy food gives them what they need.

Carbohydrates in Dog Food

Carbohydrates can make up 40 to 55 percent of dry diets and typically come from cereal grains processed for palatability and digestibility.

Typical sources of carbohydrates found in dog foods include:

- barley
- cereal grain
- corn
- corn gluten meal
- dried skim milk
- dried whey
- milling products
- milk products
- oats
- oatmeal
- rice
- rice hulls
- wheat
- wheat middlings
- fiber

We saved fiber for the end of the list because fiber is a general term for complex carbohydrates typically not digested in the dog's small intestine. Some fibers can be partially degraded by the normal function of the large intestine. We probably don't need to get into really graphic detail here, suffice to say dietary fiber has numerous effects within the gastrointestinal tract, including influences on how fast food moves through the intestine. The specific effects vary with the type of fiber, how it is processed and the amount fed. In general, fiber has a normalizing effect on the movement of food through the intestine, slowing the rate in animals with diarrhea and increasing it in constipation. As a protective mechanism, fiber can bind to some toxins and prevent their absorption into the bloodstream. So, some fiber is good. But again, check with your vet because too much fiber can cause adverse effects, such as loose stools, flatulence, increased stool volume and frequency, etc., etc.

more of the essential amino acids and can't be used alone to meet all of a dog's needs. It's important to balance the intake to insure dogs get all they need. For example, meat and soybean meal are both great sources of protein, but it is not until they are combined with other sources that they provide adequate protein for canine health.

Dogs can get all the protein they need from plant-based proteins, but only if the sources are processed properly and served with well-balanced amounts of the essential amino acids. Again, ask your veterinarian if the food you are feeding or plan to feed to your dog will supply all the animal's needs.

Protein Digestibility

Consider a pair of factors in evaluating the protein levels of different pet foods. The first is the amount of protein, and the second is how well that protein can be digested. The latter can be determined only by controlled feeding studies, so without working as an advertorial, it is safe to say that the bigger pet food makers with the larger budgets for research typically have the better information in this regard. Two diets may have the same protein level listed on their packages, but the results of animal digestion studies may indicate very different levels of protein digestibility. For example, a dog food that contains 21 percent protein with 85 percent digestibility would deliver equal amounts of protein as a diet containing 23 percent protein with 78 percent digestibility.

Too Much or Not Enough?

When dogs get more protein than they need, the extra protein is metabolized and used for energy. Unlike fat, the extra protein is not stored as such in the body. Still, once the demand for amino acids is met and protein reserves are filled, protein energy could potentially go to the production of fat.

On the other side of the coin, protein is an essential nutrient. Animals that don't get enough protein may show symptoms such as a depressed or decreased appetite, poor growth, weight loss, rough and dull fur, decreased immune function, lower reproductive performance and decreased milk production.

Two Groups of Minerals

Minerals fall into macro and micro categories. Macro-minerals are needed in greater amounts in the diet and are found in larger amounts in the body than micro-minerals.

Macro-Minerals

- Calcium (Ca)
- Chloride (Cl)
- Magnesium (Mg)
- Phosphorus (P)
- Potassium (K)
- Sodium (Na)
- Sulfur (S)

Micro-Minerals

- Copper (Cu)
- Iodide (I)
- Iron (Fe)
- Manganese (Mn)
- Selenium (Se)
- Zinc (Zn)

Carbohydrates

If you are into the latest human fad diets, you know about carbs. Carbohydrates come in three flavors: sugars, starches and dietary fiber. Simple sugars are the smallest sugar molecules and are easily digested and absorbed. Complex carbohydrates, or starches, are combinations of simple sugars forming long chains that require more digestion before they can be absorbed into the bloodstream. Dietary fibers are carbohydrates that are not completely digestible.

Simply put, carbohydrates are supplied by cereal grains and simple sugars, such as glucose, sucrose (table sugar) and lactose (milk sugar).

Carbohydrate digestion occurs primarily in the small intestine. Here, the complex compounds break down to glucose, which is the normal source of energy used by most cells in the body.

Dogs that eat more carbohydrates than they need can store the carbs as glycogen in the liver and muscles where it is converted to fat and stored in adipose tissues. During stress or exercise, glycogen is broken down to glucose and distributed throughout the body via the bloodstream.

Carbs provide energy, plain and simple. Dogs need carbohydrates in order to maintain their energy levels, and carbs need to be replaced within 30 minutes after vigorous exercise in order to keep dogs working at peak performance for several days in a row. This is very

When you supply good quality dog food, dogs need very few supplements. Things like this can help good food be better but check with your vet first.

important for working or hunting dogs. Feed those dogs as soon as you can after you leave the field and, the next day, they will show adequate energy. If you wait an hour after exercise to provide the food, the benefit of the carbs is not as great.

Research at Purina has also shown that pregnant dogs perform better with some carbohydrates in their diet. Conversely, pregnant dogs fed carbohydrate-free diets had problems whelping and did not deliver strong, healthy puppies. While no specific minimum requirements for carbohydrates have been determined for the diets of dogs, they provide a readily digested and metabolized source of energy.

Fat

Fats are concentrated forms of energy. Compared to protein and carbohydrates, fats contain approximately two-and-a-half times the amount of energy per pound. While fat digestion is more complex than that of protein or carbohydrates, healthy dogs can digest fats with great efficiency, using about 90 to 95 percent of the material.

Without going into great depth, most dietary fat is made up of triglycerides; a group of three fatty acids. Fatty acids are classified by the presence or absence of double bonds, the number of double bonds, the position of those bonds along the carbon chain and by their melting point.

Fats with no double bond at all are called saturated fats. Fats containing fatty acid chains with a double bond are called unsaturated fats. These may vary from a single double bond in the fatty acid molecule (monounsaturated) to fatty acids with many double bonds (polyunsaturated). Saturated fats are generally solid at room temperature, and unsaturated fats are usually liquid.

Dogs require linoleic acid only. This essential fatty acid is not made in the body but is required in very small amounts in the diet. Vegetable oils are the most potent sources of essential fatty acids for dogs. But dogs can use both animal and vegetable fat sources with almost equal efficiency to create energy.

What Does Fat Do?

First, it is a concentrated source of energy. For example, according to the folks at Purina, a pound of ground corn contains approximately 1,585 calories while a pound of animal fat contains approximately 4,100 calories. You can see that a little fat adds a whole lot of calories. Fat also supplies the essential fatty acids required by dogs for maintaining healthy skin and hair and serves as a carrier for fat-soluble vitamins. Finally, fat just tastes great to dogs.

Too Much or Not Enough?

Extra fat is generally stored in the body and, like with people, if enough fat is accumulated over time, animals will become obese. Again, as with people, all the same health problems apply and can even be multiplied. Dogs can end up with bone and joint problems and even diabetes. So, watch the weight.

Fat deficiencies are rare. Signs would include dry, coarse hair and flaky, dry and thickened skin. A synthetic diet completely devoid of fat would not keep a growing puppy alive for more than a couple weeks.

Minerals

Compared to other nutrients, which can be large and complex, minerals are relatively simple. Nutritional issues related to minerals include the amount of each in the diet, proper balance of all minerals and the availability of minerals in the dog food.

Minerals perform many different functions in the body, such as bone and cartilage formation, enzymatic reactions, maintaining fluid balance, transportation of oxygen in the blood, normal muscle and nerve function and the production of hormones. It is impossible to adequately nourish a dog without providing all the minerals in their proper proportions.

As always, a good quality dog food will provide all the right minerals in the right amounts for your dog. But, again, check with your vet to find out if your dog needs something special. Providing a mineral supplement should only be done under the direction of a veterinarian because supplements can cause mineral imbalances, which could create health problems for the dog.

In a dog's diet, phosphorus and calcium are essential for normal bone and tooth development. They also help with blood coagulation, aid in controlling passage of fluids to cell walls and are necessary for nerve excitability. A deficiency of calcium or phosphorus during the first year of a puppy's life will produce bone weakness and/or serious skeletal deformities, like rickets. So feed puppies good quality food from reputable makers and feed according to package instructions or veterinary directions. Don't take chances with your puppy.

Sodium and chloride are fluid-regulating minerals helping to balance fluids inside and outside individual cells. Sodium helps transfer nutrients to cells and helps remove waste material. It also helps to achieve water balance among the tissues and organs. Chloride is required for the formation of hydrochloric acid in the stomach to digest protein.

Commercial pet foods provide all the sodium and chloride dogs need, but deficiencies can result from severe diarrhea or vomiting. Such conditions require the help of a veterinarian. If a dog gets more sodium and chloride than it needs, the extra is filtered through the kidneys and excreted into the urine. Problems from too much sodium and chloride are unlikely as long as dogs have plenty of good quality drinking water.

Potassium is found within cells and is needed for proper enzyme, muscle, and nerve functions, as well as helping to maintain fluid balance throughout the body. Much like sodium and chloride, it is found in most foods and problems of too much or too little are rarely seen, except in cases of diarrhea and vomiting.

Magnesium is a structural component of both muscle and bone. It also plays a key role in many enzymatic reactions throughout the body. Calcium and phosphorus can have an impact on the magnesium balance in dogs because high amounts of calcium or phosphorus decrease the absorption of magnesium from the intestinal tract. Good quality dog food means such problems are rarely seen.

A little bit of iron goes a long way. Dogs' bodies contain only about 0.004 percent iron, but it plays a central role. Iron is needed to make hemoglobin, which carries oxygen in red blood cells. More than half the iron a dog's body has is located in the hemoglobin.

Anemia is a well-known result of a deficiency of iron. The symptoms include weakness, slow growth and inability to fight off disease. Nutritional anemia is unusual with modern dog foods and feeding supplemental iron to a nursing female won't help the puppies since doing so does not increase the iron content of the milk.

Too much iron will form insoluble phosphate and interfere with phosphorus absorption.

Of the other minerals, selenium is one of the few nutrients known to be toxic before it was found to be an essential nutrient. It is required in the smallest amount of any of the generally accepted trace elements, and it is also the most toxic. Selenium works primarily in conjunction with vitamin E to act as an antioxidant in the body.

Selenium poisoning in dogs is rare, but could occur if the intake exceeded 2 ppm (parts per million) for long periods of time. Symptoms include anemia, hair loss, soreness and weakness.

Vitamins

The study of vitamins is only about 100 years old, but already this science has had a huge impact on nutrition for both dogs and humans. This is especially interesting considering that of all the nutrients, vitamins are the ones required in the smallest amounts. Your dog doesn't need much in the way of vitamins, but the ones required are vitally important.

Vitamins are classified as either fat-soluble (vitamins A, D, E, K) or water-soluble (B-vitamins and vitamin C). Fat-soluble vitamins depend on the presence of dietary fat and normal fat absorption in order for the body to use them. Water-soluble vitamins, obviously, need water to get into the body.

Like so many of the other nutrients, vitamins do not work alone. As such, balanced diet is important. Providing extra vitamins, especially when you are already feeding a good quality dog food, will end up doing more harm than good. For example, eggs contain lots of protein, and most dogs will happily eat eggs. But you see, raw egg whites contain an enzyme that destroys the vitamin biotin. And one of the symptoms of biotin deficiency is the loss of hair. So all you people who are giving your dog raw eggs for a shiny coat, stop it. There are plenty of other examples, and plenty of other severe symptoms your veterinarian will be happy to discuss with you.

The long and short of it is this: Good dog food should provide all the vitamins your dog needs. Unless you see symptoms of a deficiency and get advice from a competent veterinarian, you don't need to give your dog extra vitamins.

Fat-Soluble Vitamins
Vitamin A

Vitamin A is likely the most studied vitamin in the area of canine health and plays a big part in areas of growth, immune system function, reproduction and normal vision. One of the great things about vitamin A is that dogs can store it in the liver for use if a change in diet requires the use of reserves.

On the down side, too much vitamin A will cause deformed bones, weight loss, anorexia and even death. Don't give vitamin A supplements without a veterinarian's order.

Vitamin D

Vitamin D is one of three major hormones involved in the regulation of calcium in the body. Vitamin D can come from food or it can be converted in the skin by exposure to sunlight. Without enough vitamin D, puppies end up with rickets, a disease where the bones remain soft or become easily broken.

Too much vitamin D for a long time could cause hardening of the heart and kidneys.

Vitamin E

Vitamin E works with other nutrients (selenium, a micro-mineral and cysteine, an amino acid) to minimize damage to cells from oxidation — thus the term antioxidant. Lack of vitamin E could result in damage to the walls of cells throughout the body. There is also a problem with too much vitamin E in dogs.

Vitamin K

Vitamin K comes from green, leafy plants and vegetables and works primarily as a clotting agent within the blood. Dogs need so little vitamin K that, according to researchers at Purina, a natural deficiency has never been reported.

Water-Soluble Vitamins

B-complex vitamins — B1, B2, B6, B12 and the others listed below— are essential to help the body use other nutrients to create energy. Unlike the fat-soluble vitamins, the B vitamins are not stored in the body. That means dogs need them every day. Good commercial dog food supplies all the B vitamins a dog needs. There could be trouble for dogs that are fed exclusively homemade food. Signs that your dog is not getting enough of the B vitamins can include loss of appetite, poor growth, weakness, weight loss and even death.

Water-Soluble B Vitamins

- Thiamin (B1)
- Niacin
- Riboflavin (B2)
- Pantothenic acid
- Pyridoxine (B6)
- Biotin
- Vitamin B12
- Choline
- Folic acid
- Inositol

Vitamin C

Dogs don't need vitamin C. It is not required for any canine bodily function. Giving a dog vitamin C is a waste of time and money.

That is the crash course on canine nutrition, and it always comes with the warning: Most of us dog owners are not veterinarians. But we do know when our dogs are not looking or acting just right. It is then we need to pay special attention to what goes in and what comes out of the dog. The latter part may not be pleasant, but it is important.

In many cases it is not an over-simplification to say that feeding a good-quality dog food is usually all you need to do to stay on the right track for proper canine nutrition. Most of the big-name pet food companies provide great products. Most of the cheap, store-brand stuff includes lots of filler and may not be processed to provide maximum nutritional benefit for your dog. You will certainly be cleaning up more poop when you feed cheap dog food, and for some people that is enough of an incentive to get the good stuff.

But more importantly, a dog that lives with a well-balanced diet and is neither overweight nor too skinny, has a far less chance of developing serious health problems. Good food, plenty of water and lots of training and attention are all most dogs really need. ⌒

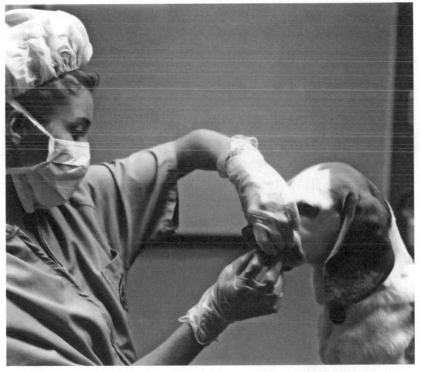

A good relationship with your vet can catch many problems before they get serious.

Chapter 14

Tips for a Happy Dog

Basic dog care is not really something that comes from the pages of a book. Sure, there are tips and tricks experienced dog owners and trainers can give you, but by and large, the way you take care of your dog is up to you and it tells a lot about you.

The first—and most important thing—you need to remember about taking care of a dog is: Your dog depends on you for everything.

That's a simple statement with just seven words, but the reality is far more complex because of that last word. Think about it. Your dog needs you for everything. From food, water and shelter to medical care, training and exercise to bathroom privileges and entertainment, your dog, in large part because of your training, is dependent on you. There's no denying it—no way to get around the facts. Once you have a dog, there's nothing you can do to change the facts, short of getting rid of the animal. And even if you choose to get rid of your dog, he is counting on you to find him a good home where he can get all the things you couldn't give.

When people say owning a dog is a big responsibility, they are correct. It's not quite as big of a responsibility as raising children, but it's close. So, I'll try to give you a short primer on basic pet care. True, many of you will say, "I already know that," but I believe it's important to issue timely reminders, especially for people who are busy with other aspects of life. Sometimes, dogs become secondary. I make no judgment about that since I also have to find time to balance work, family life, home maintenance, car repairs and dog ownership responsibilities. But if you just remember why you got the dog in the first place, that knowledge often makes it a bit easier to do everything you need to do to keep your dog healthy.

Your goal: To keep yourself and your dog happy.

What you'll need: All kinds of stuff, like dog food, a leash, patience… anything that will make life easier for your dog and you.

It's pretty easy to keep a dog happy. Food, water and some attention are about all it takes.

Do you remember why you got the dog?

If you break it down to its most basic element, nine out of 10 people buy a dog so the animal can provide happiness. With that in mind, let's talk about keeping your dog happy and healthy.

Right from the List

Food

All dogs have to eat and there are marketing managers across this country who know that. It seems everyone is trying to sell you food that's better for your dog or tastes better or is easier to digest. Remember that TV commercial with the tiny little wagon that would lead the dogs to the kitchen? You've got to cut through some of the hype. Not all of it, but some of it.

Read Chapter 13 for the medical and scientific aspects.

Your average dog will eat just about any food you put in front of him. But that doesn't mean such food will be nutritionally complete.

The cheapest dog food you can buy is just that. It's usually nothing but a lot of filler, some corn meal and a binding agent to make it all stick together. As frugal as I am, I'll regularly spend the long dollar on premium quality dog food. There are a couple of good reasons to spend more, above and beyond the fact that better food is better for the dog. Good-quality food makes your life easier in two ways: less poop and less shedding. It's true. Give your dog some bargain dog food, measure the amount and serve up two cups a day. Then make a note of how many times your dog defecates. With a top-quality food, your dog will go once a day, and you may actually end up feeding him less food because with more in each bite he's able to digest, he won't need as much food to maintain his weight. The same is true of shedding. Good dog food means a healthier coat and less hair floating around your house and car.

Go to your vet and see what food is sold in the office. Buy a small bag and see how your dog handles it. If you really need to spend less on dog food, read the ingredients carefully on the premium bag and then go to your local discount store to see which national brand most closely matched both the ingredients and the percentages of protein, fat, moisture and crude fiber. Buy that food and you should be doing pretty well for your dog.

Follow the recommendations on the bag concerning feeding amounts, but also pay attention to how much exercise your dog gets and the animal's weight. You want to keep the dog's energy level up, but you also don't want to see your dog packing on the pounds. If your dog spends time outdoors in the winter, you'll want to supply a bit more food (but water is also of major importance then, as detailed later in this chapter). If the animal is working as a doorstop or a footrest in an air-conditioned apartment, cut back on the food a bit.

Feeding time can be a challenge. Puppies and dogs that are being housebroken need to get several small meals each day. You can get away with feeding healthy adult dogs one meal per day, but you may decide you want to set a meal schedule, especially if your dog is overweight. If your hound could lose a pound, go with a couple smaller meals each day, which will help change the dog's metabolism and help the animal burn up more of the food she's eaten.

Good quality food and clean, fresh water are the keys to caring for a dog.

Water

This is the key element in your dog's diet. Once the animal is housebroken, there's really not much need to restrict water, and in some instances, you'll want to ensure the dog has all the water it wants.

Everyone knows dogs want water when it's hot outside. Dogs can't sweat, so they expel excess heat through their mouths by panting. With that heat goes a lot of moisture, meaning a dog can quickly dehydrate just by lying around panting in the heat.

On the other end of the spectrum is the water needed when a dog gets cold. There is nothing more important in keeping a dog warm during the winter than ample water. The water helps the dog digest and metabolize the food she has eaten. With no water, the interior furnace shuts down and even a dog with a belly full of food will get cold. I have dogs that live outside all year, and the first thing I buy with a new dog is an electrically heated water bucket. For years I was chipping ice and providing fresh water about four times a day during the winter months. The electric bucket means I only need to refresh the water once a day, and it will never be frozen.

A kennel need not be a palace, but is should be large, clean and include some shade.

While it's true that a thirsty dog will drink just about anything, your dog shouldn't have to settle for anything less than clean, fresh water. Make sure you keep the water dish clean and filled with water daily. Keeping the dish clean means you have to wash it once in a while. Use a good-quality cleaner to disinfect the bowl at least twice a month; once a week is better. Keeping the bowl filled with fresh water means just that. Dogs have trouble drinking from shallow dishes. Have you ever watched a dog closely as he laps up water? The dog's tongue curls under toward his lower jaw as he pulls a bit of water up into his mouth. It's not very efficient and it's even less so when drinking from very shallow water bowls. So, make it easy for your dog with a dish that is big enough and one that is clean and filled with fresh water.

Shelter

"In the doghouse" should not be a negative term. Your dog needs a place to call his own, and you can make such a place as splendid or austere as you like, as long as you make it comfortable.

There are two kinds of dogs in the world: inside dogs and outside dogs. Outside dogs need different things than inside dogs do, but they don't automatically need more things. If you plan to keep your dog outside (and that's perfectly acceptable), the best thing you can do is provide a kennel with a bit of room to roam. Most home centers sell complete chain-link kennels in various sizes for less than $200. My recommendation is to buy a kennel that is 6 feet tall. Even if you have a relatively small dog, the 4-foot kennel means you'll be ducking and banging your head every time you go in to clean out the kennel, feed the dog or change the water. A kennel that is 12 feet long, 6 feet wide and 6 feet tall will be fine for just about any dog. You can use compacted gravel, concrete patio blocks or poured concrete for the floor; just make sure it is something you can clean easily. For that matter, poured concrete is the best.

Inside the kennel, you'll want an insulated doghouse that's equipped with a windproof door that provides easy access for cleaning. There are plenty of injection-molded plastic models available. Or, if you are handy, the same home center that sold you the kennel will be happy

Do you need a small package? A cocker spaniel takes up very little space and provides unending devotion. Who could turn down that face?

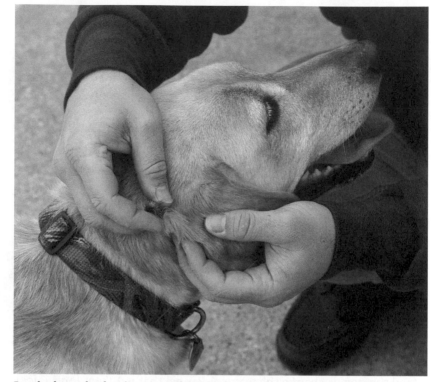

Burdocks and other items stuck in the fur can cause irritation. Take care of this quickly. If your dog has long hair, teach the animal to sit still for the brush.

Regular care should include checking the dog's pads and nails. A dog's feet take far more abuse than any other part of the animal.

to sell you a doghouse kit, a set of plans or lumber to allow you to build a house in any style you want.

If you plan to equip your kennel with an electrically heated water bucket (something I really suggest), you'll need to get a piece of conduit to shield the electric cord, just in case your dog gets bored and decides to chew on something besides the doghouse. Wire the conduit along the outside of one of the vertical support poles, allowing only enough electric cord exposed to plug in the heated bucket.

For any kennel, make sure you have a secure latch. A lockable secure latch is even better. The lock not only ensures the dog will not be able to flip the latch, but also provides some added security if anyone decides you have a really great dog they just happen to want to take.

As for inside dogs, just about anything goes. But one thing you need to provide is a portable kennel in an out-of-the-way place where the dog can go to avoid the noise and pace of an active household. Equip the portable kennel with a good-quality doggie bed and set a schedule to clean the bed regularly.

Most dog owners forget about a canine first-aid kit. The kit doesn't need to be huge, but if you need a bandage, nothing else will do.

Depending on your personal preferences, your housedog can have as many or as few restrictions as you see fit. Just remember to be consistent. Early in my marriage, my wife and I owned a happy little cocker spaniel. (Is there any other kind?) At first, there was a strict rule against allowing the dog on any furniture—especially the bed. After my first business trip, the dog looked at me like I was insane when I ordered her off the bed. From that day forward, the dog staked her claim on any piece of furniture that happened to be in a warm or sunny spot.

Housedogs need food and water like any other dog, but they also need protection from household products that can cause harm or even death. If your dog has the run-of-the-house, be sure to keep things like household cleaners, chemicals and other products secured in a cabinet or a room that is off-limits to the dog. Other than that, you can give the dog anything indoors. All you need to do is to make sure you get the dog outside for exercise and potty breaks.

Medical Care

As with anything in life, there are two ways to look at medical care for your dog: reactive or preventative. The latter is better and will help keep your vet bills lower and your dog healthier. Sure, there will be times when you need to take immediate emergency action, but if you have established a good schedule of check-ups, your vet will be familiar with your dog and you'll be familiar with the vet. It just makes things easier.

When talking about preventative medical care, you can't overlook shots. Each municipality in the country is likely to have different requirements, but all will require that your dog be vaccinated against rabies and distemper. Ask your vet to put your dog on a regular schedule; most will mail a postcard when it's time for shots. Follow the schedule faithfully and ask a lot of questions. Is there anything else your dog needs to be vaccinated against? What about Lyme disease? Or kennel cough? Be informed and get your dog everything it needs.

Another concern is heartworm. Where there are mosquitoes, your dog is exposed to potentially fatal infection of heartworms. Until recently, veterinarians would prescribe heartworm medication only during the warm months of the year. Lately though, there has been

Kids need to learn about dogs at a young age. This not only helps the children overcome any fear, it teaches them how to properly take care of their own pets in the future.

a push for year-round defense against these deadly invaders. It only costs a little bit more to keep the dog on heartworm medicine year-round, so for the sake of your pet, buy the extra pills and administer them every month.

The long and short of preventive medicine is to get on your vet's mailing list and follow directions as they are given. I'm not telling you not to ask questions; just don't skimp on regular care for your pet. These regular visits can also aid in early detection of other diseases. It's really all about common sense.

If you have an active dog and you get outside a lot, sooner or later, you'll need to deal with some minor injuries or make an emergency trip to the vet. You need to be ready for just such an eventuality. People tend to look at me a little bit funny when I say that I maintain a doggie first-aid kit in addition to the human model I keep in my house. But why not have one? I can't think of a good reason to do without it.

As you would guess, medical care for dogs is a bit different than tending to the bumps, scrapes and cuts that most often require services provided from a human first-aid kit. I've found two items most important in my canine first aid kit: Vetrap and a pair of locking forceps.

Vetrap is the brand name of a clingy, bandage material made by 3M Company. The stuff is almost self-adhesive without being sticky like tape. It's just the stuff you need if your dog suffers a cut that's big enough to require a bandage. Put some gauze over the cut, wrap with a couple layers of Vetrap and take the dog for an exam.

The locking forceps are needed because I live and travel in porcupine country. One encounter with a porcupine proved the need for some forceps. Future encounters were no less stressful, but the tool really made my first-aid much easier.

Other items included in the doggie first-aid kit are:

- sterile saline solution to be used as eyewash or to irrigate cuts before bandaging
- gauze pads
- triple antibiotic ointment
- a lightweight muzzle (In only one instance did I not have a dog try to bite me as I administered medical care, and that dog had so many porcupine quills in his tongue, lips and nose that he seemed to know I was just there to help.)

If your dog gets hurt, the first thing you need to do is get control of him. Snap on the leash, and just as a precaution, put on the muzzle. The next step is to get some help. Most dogs don't like to sit still when they are hurt. You'll need at least one person to restrain and attempt to calm the dog while you get to work. Once you've got the initial problem solved, get the dog to a veterinarian to make sure everything is fine.

Training

This has been the basis of the whole book. Read the chapters presented here and make training a habit. Get on a schedule and adhere to it. I can't repeat enough that a well-trained dog will make your ownership responsibilities that much easier and provide even more enjoyment as a pet.

Dogs love to get together, but it always pays to keep control of the animals until they get acquainted.

Exercise

A dog might not always get enough exercise from your training sessions. Plan to include walks, runs and swimming in your scheduled outings, but do it wisely.

Walking and running can be hard on a dog's feet. If you have a housedog and suddenly decide that it's time she becomes a little more active, don't just snap on the leash and take off on an hour walk around town. It will take a series of short trips to help the dog's muscles get used to the exercise, but more importantly, it will take time to toughen up the pads on a dog's feet. Even hard-working dogs get sore feet. A housedog used to a life of leisure will have soft pads, and you'll often see the dog licking his feet after a long walk. Don't stop exercising because of this; just shorten up the trips for a while until the dog's feet get in shape.

If you run or jog and you want to take your dog along, you don't have to worry so much about how far and fast you run, but you do need to think about your route. Are you running on gravel trails, sidewalks, along busy streets or up and down steep hills? Will you have your dog on a leash or will you require the animal to trot at your side? Do you need to carry water for your dog? Are there other dogs along the way? Are you able and willing to stop and scoop poop in the middle of your run?

You won't be totally building your workout around the dog, but you will be changing it to accommodate the fact that a dog is coming along with you. As every person and every dog is different, you'll need to experiment and tailor that route and the workout to what works for both you and the dog. It might be a good idea to carry a fanny pack with some water, a leash and perhaps a muzzle. Plan for the unexpected.

Swimming is another great activity for a dog, but not all dogs are born as strong swimmers. If you throw a ball or a dummy 10 yards into the water 10 times, your dog is going to swim 200 yards. That's a lot of exercise. Don't overdo it.

As with any human exercise program, once you get started it's important to keep your dog involved. These exercise trips might become part of your dog's routine, and if they are suddenly abandoned, you could end up with a dog that needs to release some extra energy by barking all day or chewing your furniture.

If you need to, protect your dog from over-active kids. In this case, Echo not only tolerates Adam, she loves the attention.

This is what it's all about. You can have a dog that you trust completely, one that will do what you say when you say it, with just 15 minutes of training each day.

Entertainment

Let's face it: Dogs are here for our entertainment. They are fun to play with and we enjoy having them around, but they are not toys. I often feel the need to remind people, especially those with young children, that dogs get tired, bored and sometimes just want to be left alone. In short, dogs can have too much fun. That's why it's so important to give them a safe and secure place to get away from it all. But even more important than that is to be able to recognize when the dog wants to be alone and to respond accordingly. That could mean telling your nieces and nephews to "leave Buffy alone for a while."

If you're planning a big gathering, or even a small one involving people your dog is not familiar with, make sure the animal has ready access to an "escape route" that is off-limits to your human guests—especially children. You don't have to have "pre-party huddle" or post a list of doggie rules, but take some time to let people know what's going on as it becomes appropriate.

Make sure you've done your homework getting ready for a dog before you
get to this point. Once something like this happens, you've already bought
the dog, even if you don't know it yet.

Some events that require special attention include any gathering that involves dancing and loud music, active outdoor games like volleyball, softball or soccer, and groups of people who like to get loud and laugh a lot. You can invite the dog into these groups, but watch the animal's body language. If the dog is cowering or growling, get that animal back into the portable kennel. Also, if the games are going on outside and the dog is running around looking confused, try to get him out of the melee. Place a favorite chew toy in the kennel and secure the door. Just remember to go back and check on the dog occasionally, because this type of activity can upset the dog's regular rhythms concerning potty breaks. If the dog seems stressed and agitated while in the kennel, take a few minutes to let the dog out (on the leash, of course) before you return to the party.

Also, if your dog is not accustomed to having children around, don't subject the animal to the happy hands of the little ones. Kids are great, but they are tough on dogs, and the younger the kid, the tougher it is for the dog to put up with the little guy's "playing." You never want to leave your dog in a situation where continued poking, prodding and playing could result in a youngster getting bit. It gives the dog an often-undeserved bad reputation and can cost you (or your homeowners' insurance carrier) some serious cash.

It's best to keep kids and dogs closely monitored and to give the children very direct instructions concerning the dog. You'll very likely want to encourage a good relationship between the youngster and the dog and the best way to do that is to control the child every bit as much as you control the dog.

One of the best things you can do for kids and dogs is to sit down with both of them and soothe the dog while you explain every little thing and answer every question the child has. Show the youngster how the dog likes to be petted and point out that the dog's ears, eyes and nose are very sensitive. Tell the child that if the dog gets up to walk away, that means he's done playing and wants to be left alone. Never let a child follow a dog that's trying to move away. The dog only wants to create some space and be left alone. An overly persistent youngster might just make the dog angry. Step in and stop that before it gets out of hand.

The Last Word

Finally, people can—and have—written entire books on basic dog care, but the truth is, they are all about opinion. If you look long enough, you can find a book that supports your ideas of how you should take care of your dog. Don't ever discount your beliefs or God-given common sense. If you are providing food, water, shelter and basic but effective training, you are on the right track to having a healthy and happy dog.

The only other thing you need to concentrate on is kindness. Think of your dog as your friend. Provide your training, even your corrections, consistently. Be kind and patient, but persistent, and your dog will respond to your training quickly and will remain happy and well-adjusted.

If you think something you're doing isn't quite right, go with your gut. If you still have questions, ask your veterinarian. Most of the time you'll find out you were right all along, and you just needed that affirmation to prove that you were on the right track.

Dog training doesn't have to be difficult, and dog care doesn't have to be demanding. You can have a great dog with just 15 minutes of training per day, plus a little bit of extra time for fun. If you follow that basic schedule, you'll see that dog ownership provides more benefits than you could have imagined.

Once you've established that the parents are good dogs, any of these little guys would make a great companion. Don't think about just the pups before you buy, because, as you can see, they're all cute.

Chapter 15

A Review of Popular Breeds

Akita

Temperament: While affectionate with its family, the Akita is very aggressive to other dogs. Intelligent, and fearless, it is a first-class guard dog but needs firm training as a puppy. Extremely faithful and enjoys companionship.
Health Issues: Prone to immune diseases, like VKH and hip dysplasia.
Life Span: 10-12 years.
Housing and Exercise: Will do well in an apartment if it is exercised often. It is active indoors and will do best with a large yard.

Alaskan Malamute

Temperament: Friendly, good-natured breed that is usually good with children

and strangers. Strong-willed and confident; tends to be very stubborn and early obedience training is a must.
Health Issues: Susceptible to hip dysplasia, and eye problems.
Life Span: 10-12 years.
Housing and Exercise: Needs lots of space. A house with a large fenced yard with some shade is essential.

American Bulldog

Temperament: Outstandingly obedient and truly loyal to his master if trained properly. Eager to please, and genuinely loves children. Known to be assertive and bold. Happiest when he has a job to do.
Health Issues: Prone to hip dysplasia.
Life Span: Up to 16 years.
Housing and Exercise:
Inactive indoors and requires a yard and moderate exercise outside.

American Pit Bull Terrier

Temperament: With proper training, can be loyal and well mannered. But has been known to be aggressive, especially to other dogs. When properly socialized, makes good family pet and intimidating guard dog.

Health Issues: Usually healthy, but some may be allergic to grass.

Life Span: About 12 years.

Housing and Exercise: A good fence is called for. Has lots of energy and needs supervision. Only as good as her owner.

Australian Shepherd

Temperament: Intelligent, clever and devoted. Eager to please and easy to train. Affectionate and active; makes an excellent children's companion.

Health Issues: Susceptible to hip dysplasia, blindness and deafness.

Life Span: 12-15 years.

Housing and Exercise: Needs frequent exercise and always does best with room to roam. Happiest when it has a job to do, whether it's herding sheep or keeping an eye on kids. Great breed for agility or obedience training and competition.

Basset Hound

Temperament: Fits well into family life and is well-behaved, but it may be stubborn. With proper training, they are obedient, but when they pick up scent, they may not listen to commands.

Health Issues: Do not overfeed because extra weight places a load on the legs and spine that can leave the dog lame. Prone to bloat.

Life Span: 10-12 years.

Housing and Exercise: Will do okay in an apartment, but very inactive indoors. Outdoors, expect hours of play. Exercise is needed to keep them healthy and trim, but in moderation—with their short legs, walking is much better than running.

Beagle

Temperament: Has a cheerful, upbeat personality and is great with kids. Like all scent hounds, is independent and will always "follow their noses"—ignoring your protests to return. Teach the dog to come early.

Health Issues: Susceptible to epilepsy, glaucoma and heart disease.

Life Span: 12-15 years.

Housing and Exercise: Needs companionship and daily exercise. Bred to hunt and drive game and may be difficult to break of that. Prone to barking and howling; do not make good apartment dogs.

Bernese Mountain Dog

Temperament: Gets along well with, and is extremely loyal to, her family and often attaches herself to one member. Eager to please and easy to train. Intelligent and loving and loving and makes an excellent family dog. May be slow to mature and have puppy-like habits well after other dogs have "grown up."

Health Issues: Can suffer from hip dysplasia, hereditary eye diseases, intestinal disorders and cancer.

Life Span: About 6-8 years.

Housing and Exercise:
Not a dog for apartments. Requires a large yard in a cooler climate.

Bichon Frise

Temperament: Very perky and playful. Gets along well with strangers, small children and other dogs and pets, but will often bark a lot.

Health Issues: Susceptible to skin and ear problems, epilepsy and leg problems.

Life Span: 12-15 years.

Housing and Exercise: Does well in apartments, but should be walked about twice a day.

Boxer

Temperament: Energetic, attentive and devoted dog that is gentle with children. Behaves well with other household pets, but cautious with strange pets and people. Can make good guard dog.

Health Issues:
Susceptible to hip dysplasia, cancer (in older dogs), allergies and heart problems .

Life Span: 8-10 years.

Housing and Exercise: Full of energy;

perfect companion for active families. Requires mental and physical exertion and not recommended for people who are easy going and slow moving. Sensitive to hot and cold weather. Does best when allowed to divide time between the house and the yard.

Brittany

Temperament: Highly energetic and friendly. Good-natured. Does well with children and other pets. Can be soft; harsh training is not recommended.

Health Issues: Susceptible to hip dysplasia and seizures.

Life Span: 12-13 years.

Housing and Exercise: Very energetic; enjoys a big yard. Gets nervous if not given enough exercise. An excellent breed for the hunter who also wants a family pet.

Bulldog

Temperament: Friendly and good-natured—an almost mellow dog that is very good with children. May be aggressive with strange dogs, but usually gets along well with other pets.

Health Issues: Susceptible to breathing and whelping difficulties, and overheating.

Life Span: 8-10 years.

Housing and Exercise: Needs little exercise to remain happy. Good apartment dogs; a walk each day will provide enough exercise. Should not be made to run or walk long distances in hot weather.

Cavalier King Charles Spaniel

Temperament: Gentle dogs that will cower if treated heavily. Respond much better to positive training. A lap dog that, given a choice, would always choose the company of groups of people.

Health Issues: Susceptible to breathing problems, heart disease (MVD), eye problems and ear infections.

Life Span: 10-12 years.

Housing and Exercise: Needs very little exercise. Should also be kept away from very hot or extremely cold conditions.

Chesapeake Bay Retriever

Temperament: Protective breed that will serve as a solid watchdog—yet is loyal to family and easy to train. Makes a good family pet if raised from a pup in a loving home with firm rules.

Health Issues: Susceptible to eye diseases and hip dysplasia.

Life Span: 10-13 years.

Housing and Exercise: Inactive indoors. Bred to hunt the icy waters of Chesapeake Bay; deserves to be challenged physically. Should sleep outdoors because that's what it likes.

Chihuahua

Temperament: Makes a wonderful companion, but is sometimes timid around new people—because of this, makes a good watchdog.

Health Issues: Susceptible to leg and eye problems.

Life Span: 15 or more years.

Housing and Exercise: Takes well to apartment life, but can be noisy. Needs little exercise, but very playful.

Chow Chow

Temperament: Smart and protective. Most will be loyal to only a few people, and likely to be very aggressive toward other dogs. The owner should be an experienced dog handler and be prepared to handle this sometimes stubborn and aggressive breed.

Health Issues: Like most bigger dogs, can suffer hip dysplasia.

Life Span: 8-12 years.

Housing and Exercise: Needs lots of exercise and should be fenced to help keep them from other dogs.

Cocker Spaniel

Temperament: Lovable little dogs. Perfect for the whole family, but can become jealous when new children are brought into the home.

Health Issues: Sometimes suffer from ear

infections, hip dysplasia and epilepsy. Find a reputable breeder and watch for eye trouble.

Life Span: 12-15 years.

Housing and Exercise: Adapts well to any environment, but needs plenty of exercise. Loves to chase tennis balls.

Collie

Temperament: Highly intelligent, sensitive, loyal and easy to train. Usually tolerates other dogs. Very devoted.

Health Issues: Generally healthy, but some are prone to PRA, eye defects and hip problems leading to arthritis.

Life Span: 14-16 years.

Housing and Exercise: Will do well in an apartment with plenty of exercise. Provide shade and fresh water in warm weather. Inactive indoors; needs a yard.

Dachshund

Temperament: Defined by their coats: smooth-haired are typically friendly; longhaired can be leery of strangers; and wirehaired can be stubborn.

Health Issues: Susceptible to eye diseases and skin problems.

Life Span: 12-14 years.

Housing and Exercise: Can sometimes be noisy, but will live in apartments as long as they get lots of exercise and attention.

Dalmatian

Temperament: Loves his owner, but can be tough to train because he gets so excited at times.

Health Issues: Many are deaf thanks to indiscriminate breeding. Can also suffer urinary tract problems and skin ailments.

Life Span: 12-14 years.

Housing and Exercise: Loves to run and play. Get ready to put on your walking shoes—these dogs need to get out and move around.

Doberman Pinscher

Temperament: Intense, intelligent and energetic, yet easy to train. Assertive, but not vicious. Still, all family members should be able to handle the dog. Should be thoroughly socialized.

Health Issues: Generally healthy, but prone to bloat, hip dysplasia, congenital heart disorders and obesity in middle age.

Life Span: 11-13 years.

Housing and Exercise: Very cold sensitive; not an outside dog. Will do well in an apartment if exercised.

English Springer Spaniel

Temperament: Another true family dog. A quick learner that loves people.
Health Issues: Can suffer epilepsy, ear infections and eye problems.
Life Span: 10-14 years.
Housing and Exercise: Should have daily exercise. As a dog developed for hunting upland game, has boundless energy that should be put to good use.

Fox Terrier

Temperament: Can be playful and loving, or feisty and quick to bite. Supervise this dog around children and other pets. Make excellent watchdogs because they bark a lot.
Health Issues: Prone to epilepsy and shoulder problems. Very light-colored dogs show higher rates of deafness.
Life Span: 15 or more years.
Housing and Exercise: Bred to hunt and will chase smaller animals—walk on a leash every day.

German Shepherd Dog

Temperament: Highly intelligent, territorial, devoted and faithful. Initially suspicious of strangers. A great watchdog that can be trained to handle just about any job.
Life Span: 10-12 years.
Health Issues: Susceptible to skin disease, bloat, heart problems and hip dysplasia.

Enormous popularity has led to careless breeding, resulting in a number of crippling genetic problems within the breed. Look for a reputable breeder.
Housing and Exercise: Needs exercise and daily mental challenges. Makes good housedog, although a fenced yard and plenty of stimulation is required.

German Shorthaired Pointer

Temperament: A ball of energy and intelligence. Makes a good family dog, but sometimes rough with small children and smaller pets. Like most pointers, likes to roam and search.
Health Issues: Bigger dogs are susceptible to hip dysplasia. Can also suffer epilepsy. Because of the popularity of the dog, look for a good breeder.
Life Span: 12-14 years.
Housing and Exercise: Needs to hunt. Can live in the city, but offer lots of exercise and games.

Giant Schnauzer

Temperament: Great with kids when taught by an experienced trainer. Stubborn.
Health Issues: Usually very healthy.
Life Span: 12-15 years.
Housing and Exercise: Needs to play every day. Really enjoys roughhousing and running around.

Golden Retriever

Temperament: Loving and gentle. Will not take well to heavy-handed training. Great with children and can be trained to be wonderful assistance dogs.
Health Issues: Can suffer skin and thyroid problems, eye trouble and hip dysplasia.
Life Span: 10-13 years.
Housing and Exercise: Hunting dog, bred to flush and retrieve game birds. Needs challenges and active human companionship, not confinement in apartments.

Great Dane

Temperament: Despite size, is very active and plays well with children if watched closely. Tough to train; be firm.
Health Issues: Can suffer intestinal troubles, hip dysplasia and heart problems.
Life Span: 6-8 years.
Housing and Exercise: Relatively inactive inside, but often quite active outdoors. Give this giant lots of room.

Great Pyrenees

Temperament: Loyal, and a good watchdog, but difficult to train. Firmness and patience are the orders of the day.
Health Issues: Can suffer hip dysplasia and epilepsy.
Life Span: 10-12 years.
Housing and Exercise: Should have a country home, ideally with something to watch over. Needs daily exercise.

Greyhound

Temperament: Makes great companion, but can be timid. Often becomes devoted to their families. Dogs off the track are easy to housebreak and make great pets.
Health Issues: Can get sores lying on hard surfaces. Should be fed two or three small meals each day.
Life Span: 10-12 years.
Housing and Exercise: Should be allowed to run around daily. Can do well in an apartment as long as they have solid routine and exercise.

Irish Setter

Temperament: Wonderful family dog, friendly and smart. But because of their popularity, bad breeding has made some of them high-strung. Must be trained young.
Health Issues: Susceptible to bloat, epilepsy and eye problems
Life Span: 11-15 years.

Housing and Exercise: Roaming dog originally bred to range widely to find game. Loves to run and should be allowed to do so often. Make sure you teach this dog her basic commands well.

Irish Terrier

Temperament: Loves children, and will protect them with great vigor. But, doesn't like other dogs around and will fight with them given the chance. Keep on a leash to keep under control.

Health Issues: Almost always healthy.

Life Span: 12-15 years.

Housing and Exercise: Can live in an apartment, but does better with more space. Requires firm training and control, especially out in public.

Jack Russell Terrier

Temperament: Confident, but also seems to enjoy training. This attitude serves well in the field as a hunter or in the home as a playmate.

Health Issues: Typically healthy, but some dogs suffer eye problems and bad knees.

Life Span: 13-15 years.

Housing and Exercise:
Enjoys space for play, but can live in an apartment if walked daily.

Labrador Retriever

Temperament: A true all-around dog. Easy to train, great with children and willing to

do just about anything. Has found work in hunting fields, on police forces and on back porches around the world.

Health Issues: If not the product of good breeding, is susceptible to hip dysplasia, epilepsy and eye diseases.

Life Span: 10-12 years.

Housing and Exercise: Needs to work to be happy and healthy. Loves to find things and fetch them, especially in the water. A very capable and versatile hunting companion, or a great partner for just about any kind of outdoor activity.

Lhasa Apso

Temperament: Very friendly and smart, but dislikes strangers and makes an excellent watchdog.

Health Issues: Sometimes suffers from hip dysplasia and skin, kidney and eye problems.

Life Span: 12-14 years.

Housing and Exercise: Can be very active indoors. A walk each day will provide plenty of exercise.

Mastiff

Temperament: Bred as a watchdog that will be happy and friendly with family members.

Health Issues: Because of their large size, are susceptible to bone and heart problems. Some dogs suffer from bloat, depending on their diet.

Life Span: 8-10 years.

Housing and Exercise: Does best in a house with a fenced yard. The owner should be a strong and confident leader to keep the Mastiff from becoming spoiled and pushy.

Newfoundland

Temperament: A family dog through and through. Is suspicious of strangers, but kind and caring around family members.

Health Issues: Susceptible to hip dysplasia and hereditary heart problems.

Life Span: 8-10 years.

Housing and Exercise: Needs space and

does not like too much heat. Yet, these gentle giants are very active; avoid if you live in a warm climate.

Nova Scotia Duck Tolling Retriever

Temperament: Playful, happy and easy to train. Typically barks very little and seems to really love being near children.
Health Issues: Susceptible to eye trouble and thyroid problems.
Life Span: 12-14 years.
Housing and Exercise: Having been bred on the coasts of Canada, enjoys cool weather and loves the chance to swim. Needs plenty of exercise and will fetch for as long as you are willing to throw an object.

Old English Sheepdog

Temperament: Was once actually used to herd sheep; now most often kept simply as pets. Loves to play with children and will often circle groups of kids in an effort to "herd" them.
Health Issues: Prone to hip dysplasia and cataracts.
Life Span: 10-12 years.
Housing and Exercise: Loves to play and run, and requires plenty of room. Sheds and requires plenty of grooming.

Pomeranian

Temperament: Makes a good companion and enjoys being a lap dog, but tends to bark—a lot—at strangers and other animals.
Health Issues:
Susceptible to tooth problems.
Life Span: 12-16 years.
Housing and Exercise: Suitable for all environments, whether it be in a house, apartment, city or country. Enjoys an active family atmosphere. Can be a great companion for the elderly.

Poodle (Toy)

Temperament:
Good-tempered and devoted to his family. While affectionate with their owners, can be timid with new people.
Health Issues: Susceptible to leg problems, epilepsy, ear infections, eye disease and diabetes.
Life Span: 12-14 years.
Housing and Exercise: Does well in apartments and good dog for less-active people. One walk a day is fine. Poodles come in three sizes. From largest to smallest they are: standard, miniature and toy. Standard poodles were originally retrieving dogs, but all members of the breed are now considered show dogs. There are very few working poodles left.

Portuguese Water Dog

Temperament: Intelligent. Originally bred to guard Portuguese fishing boats, carry messages and retrieve anything that fell overboard. Gets along well with children and other dogs, and is quite loyal. Responds well to tone of voice.

Health Issues: Susceptible to hip dysplasia. Breeding stock should be tested for GM-1 Storage Disease, a fatal nerve disease that appears when a puppy is 6 months old.

Life Span: 10-14 years.

Housing and Exercise: Does well in an apartment as long as it gets lots of exercise. In temperate climates can live outside, but likes to be close to people. Loves to retrieve and does not shed. Has curly hair and should be groomed often.

Rhodesian Ridgeback

Temperament: Originally bred for fighting lions. Can withstand the harsh desert heat and is not bothered by bugs. Loyal and obedient. Makes a good guard dog.

Health Issues: Susceptible to hip dysplasia, dermoid sinus and cysts.

Life Span: 10-12 years.

Housing and Exercise: Can live in an apartment, but requires tons of exercise. Seems to never get tired. Perfect if you need a watchdog and love to exercise.

Rottweiler

Temperament: Very territorial and imposing, ideal for protection. Requires strong leadership and firm training.

Health Issues: Susceptible to hip dysplasia, bloat and parvo virus. Popularity has led to careless breeding, resulting in a number of problems within the breed.

Life Span: 8-11 years.

Housing and Exercise: Needs plenty of exercise and activity. Because it dislikes newcomers, should not be kept where people often pass by.

Saint Bernard

Temperament: Very gentle and friendly, but must be obedience trained early because it gets so big. Should get daily exercise and have plenty of room to roam.

Health Issues: Susceptible to heart problems, skin problems and hip dysplasia.

Life Span: 8-10 years.

Housing and Exercise: Does best with lots of room and time spent outside. Tends to be lethargic indoors. Even so, prefers to be near people.

Scottish Terrier

Temperament: A confident little dog that that can serve as a watchdog. May be cool toward strangers and aggressive with other dogs.

Health Issues: May suffer from flea allergy and skin problems.

Life Span: 11-13 years.

Housing and Exercise: Does well in an apartment as long as it gets plenty of exercise.

Shetland Sheepdog

Temperament: Loyal, affectionate and very responsive to training. Can be shy around strangers. Alert and protective, making it a good watchdog.

Health Issues: Susceptible to Dermato-myositis (Sheltie Skin Syndrome), thyroid disease and hip dysplasia.
Life Span: 12-14 years.
Housing and Exercise: Needs daily walks and active play time, but will adapt to just about any lifestyle. Loves obedience training and competition.

Weimaraner

Temperament: Affectionate and very rambunctious. Intelligent, but can be willful, and should have firm training from the start. Socialize them well at an early age.
Health Issues: May suffer hip dysplasia, but are generally a hardy breed of dog. Prone to bloat, so feed several small meals, not one big one.
Life Span: 10- 13 years.
Housing and Exercise: Needs plenty of opportunities to run free and lots of regular exercise. Relatively inactive indoors; will do best with a large yard. Do not exercise after meals.

Welsh Corgi (Cardigan)
Temperament: A fun-loving dog that very much wants to be part of a family. Intelligent, obedient and protective; does not immediately trust strangers.
Health Issues: Susceptible to back disorders, glaucoma and epilepsy.
Life Span: 12-15 years.
Housing and Exercise: Adaptable to a

number of environments. Does well in apartments, but should be given plenty of exercise. Loves walks and playtime—fetch with a ball is a particular favorite.

Yorkshire Terrier

Temperament: Thinks it is bigger than it really is, but only up to a point. Usually timid around strangers and doesn't like rough play. Tends to bark a lot more than it should.
Health Issues: Susceptible to eye irritations, tracheal collapse, tooth problems and leg trouble.
Life Span: 14-16 years.
Housing and Exercise: Less active than other terriers, and doesn't need much exercise. But, even one long walk a day won't quiet her down if excited.

Appendix: Listing of AKC Breeds

This is the list of breeds currently recognized by the American Kennel Club. If you can't find a dog you like on this list, you might just be a cat person. There is something for everyone here. Check out www.AKC.org for information about helping you select a breed or breeder and find out more about the joys and responsibilities of owning a purebred puppy.

A

Affenpinscher
Afghan Hound
Airedale Terrier
Akita
Alaskan Malamute
American Eskimo Dog
American Foxhound
American
   Staffordshire Terrier
American Water Spaniel
Anatolian Shepherd
Australian Cattle Dog
Australian Shepherd
Australian Terrier

B

Basenji
Basset Hound
Beagle
Bearded Collie
Bedlington Terrier
Belgian Malinois
Belgian Sheepdog
Belgian Tervuren
Bernese Mountain Dog
Bichon Frise
Black and Tan
   Coonhound
Black Russian Terrier
Bloodhound
Border Collie
Border Terrier
Borzoi
Boston Terrier
Bouvier des Flandres
Boxer
Briard
Brittany
Brussels Griffon
Bull Mastiff
Bull Terrier
Bulldog

C

Cairn Terrier
Canaan Dog
Cardigan Welsh Corgi
Cavalier King
   Charles Spaniel
Chesapeake Bay
   Retriever
Chihuahua
Chinese Crested
Chinese Shar-Pei
Chow Chow
Clumber Spaniel
Cocker Spaniel
Collie
Curly-Coated Retriever

D

Dachshund
Dalmatian
Dandie Dinmont Terrier
Doberman Pinscher

E

English Cocker Spaniel
English Foxhound
English Setter
English Springer Spaniel
English Toy Spaniel

F

Field Spaniel
Finnish Spitz
Flat-Coated Retriever
French Bulldog

G

German Pinscher
German Shepherd Dog
German Shorthaired
   Pointer
German Wirehaired
   Pointer
Giant Schnauzer
Golden Retriever
Gordon Setter
Great Dane
Great Pyrenees
Greater Swiss
   Mountain Dog
Greyhound

H

Harrier
Havanese

I

Ibizan Hound
Irish Setter
Irish Terrier
Irish Water Spaniel
Irish Wolfhound
Italian Greyhound

J

Japanese Chin

K

Keeshond
Kerry Blue Terrier
Komondor
Kuvasz

L

Labrador Retriever
Lakeland Terrier
Lhasa Apso
Löwchen

M

Maltese
Manchester Terrier
Mastiff
Miniature Bull Terrier
Miniature Pinscher
Miniature Schnauzer

N

Neapolitan Mastiff
Newfoundland
Norfolk Terrier
Norwegian Elkhound
Norwich Terrier
Nova Scotia Duck
   Tolling Retriever

O

Old English Sheepdog
Otterhound

P

Papillon
Parson Russell Terrier
Pekingese
Pembroke Welsh Corgi
Petit Basset Griffon
   Vendéen
Pharaoh Hound
Pointer
Polish Lowland
   Sheepdog
Pomeranian
Poodle
Portuguese Water Dog
Pug
Puli

R

Rhodesian Ridgeback
Rottweiler

S

Saluki
Samoyed
Schipperke
Scottish Deerhound
Scottish Terrier
Sealyham Terrier
Shetland Sheepdog
Shiba Inu
Shih Tzu
Siberian Husky
Silky Terrier
Skye Terrier
Smooth Fox Terrier
Soft Coated
   Wheaten Terrier
Spinone Italiano
St. Bernard
Staffordshire Bull Terrier
Standard Schnauzer
Sussex Spaniel

T

Tibetan Spaniel
Tibetan Terrier
Toy Fox Terrier

V

Vizsla

W

Weimaraner
Welsh Springer Spaniel
Welsh Terrier
West Highland
   White Terrier
Whippet
Wire Fox Terrier
Wirehaired Pointing
   Griffon

Y

Yorkshire Terrier

Resources

Books

American Kennel Club. *The Complete Dog Book, 19th Ed.* Howell Book House, 1998.

This is probably the most popular resource for studying and comparing the traits of the 146 AKC-recognized breeds.

Benjamin, Carol Lea. *The Chosen Puppy: How to Select and Raise a Great Puppy from an Animal Shelter.* Howell House Books, 1990.

A popular handbook for people who are planning to adopt a puppy from an animal shelter—a great place to get a great dog.

Boone, Eugene. *The Big Book of Pet Names.* RSVP Press, 2004.

More than 10,000 possible names for your puppy.

Coile, D. Caroline and Michele Earle-Bridges. *Barron's Encyclopedia of Dog Breeds.* Barron's Educational Series, 1998.

A colorful and comprehensive guide to AKC breeds—a good resource for selecting the right purebred dog.

Fogle, Bruce and Amanda Williams. *First Aid for Dogs: What to Do When Emergencies Happen.* Penguin Books, 1997.

A good addition to your dog's first-aid kit.

Garvey, Michael S. DVM, et al. *The Veterinarian's Guide to Your Dog's Symptoms.* Villard, 1999.

This is a concise book that uses a flow-chart system to help dog owners analyze 150 common symptoms.

Griffin, James M., and Liisa D. Carlson. *Dog Owner's Home Veterinary Handbook.* Howell Book House, 1999.

A comprehensive, highly illustrated, easy-to-use guide to every aspect of your dog's health.

Michalowski, Kevin. *15 Minutes to a Great Puppy.* Krause Publications, 2004.

The author's companion volume focused on the training and care of puppies.

Siegal, Mordecai. *UC Davis Book of Dogs: The Complete Medical Reference for Dogs and Puppies.* HarperResources, 1995.

A comprehensive guide to dog health, growth, development, feeding and much more. Very good, but technical.

Storer, Pat. *Crate Training Your Dog.* Storey Books, 2000.

This 32-page booklet gives you quick and easy tips on house training dogs of all ages.

Internet Sites

www.aboutdogs.com

A web site devoted to all things about dogs, with several perspectives for each topic.

www.akc.org

The American Kennel Club web site. Focused on purebreds, but packed with all kinds of goodies for anybody that loves dogs.

www.dogchow.com

Great site, but with a decidedly Purina attitude. If you can ignore sales pitches, you'll be fine.

www.drsfostersmith.com

The web site of the world-famous Drs. Foster and Smith catalog—the best dog beds and everything else you need, including advice.

www.dunns.com

A dog-training supply house of the first order if you love hunting dogs and the sporting life. Nothing cheap here. This is all top-of-the-line stuff.

www.gooddogmagazine.com

Previously a print publication, now web-only. Primary focus is product test reports on dog foods and other dog products.

www.inch.com/~dogs/index.htm

The link to the American Dog Trainers Network. This site has everything. It will point you in the right direction, no matter what your question.

www.petcarerx.com

This site will give you a good look at pet medications, including some tips on use and ailments, but always check with your local vet first.

www.petplace.com

This is a fee-based web site that provides lots of information and articles from pet specialists of all types.

www.petrix.com/dognames

A simple site listing more than 2,000 possible names for your puppy.

www.thepetcenter.com

Bills itself as the Internet animal hospital. Lots of good information, but double check with a reputable vet.

www.workingdogs.com

An online "cyberzine" devoted to working and sporting dogs— sled dogs, herders, trackers, police dogs, search and rescue dogs and much more.